T0286876

Cambridge Elements ≡

Elements in Shakespeare Performance
edited by
W. B. Worthen
Barnard College

SLEEP NO MORE AND THE DISCOURSES OF SHAKESPEARE PERFORMANCE

D. J. Hopkins
San Diego State University

CAMBRIDGE
UNIVERSITY PRESS

Shaftesbury Road, Cambridge CB2 8EA, United Kingdom

One Liberty Plaza, 20th Floor, New York, NY 10006, USA

477 Williamstown Road, Port Melbourne, VIC 3207, Australia

314–321, 3rd Floor, Plot 3, Splendor Forum, Jasola District Centre, New Delhi – 110025, India

103 Penang Road, #05–06/07, Visioncrest Commercial, Singapore 238467

Cambridge University Press is part of Cambridge University Press & Assessment, a department of the University of Cambridge.

We share the University's mission to contribute to society through the pursuit of education, learning and research at the highest international levels of excellence.

www.cambridge.org
Information on this title: www.cambridge.org/9781009436892

DOI: 10.1017/9781009436908

© D. J. Hopkins 2024

This publication is in copyright. Subject to statutory exception and to the provisions of relevant collective licensing agreements, no reproduction of any part may take place without the written permission of Cambridge University Press & Assessment.

When citing this work, please include a reference to the DOI 10.1017/9781009436908

First published 2024

A catalogue record for this publication is available from the British Library.

ISBN 978-1-009-43689-2 Paperback
ISSN 2516-0117 (online)
ISSN 2516-0109 (print)

Cambridge University Press & Assessment has no responsibility for the persistence or accuracy of URLs for external or third-party internet websites referred to in this publication and does not guarantee that any content on such websites is, or will remain, accurate or appropriate.

Sleep No More and the Discourses of Shakespeare Performance

Elements in Shakespeare Performance

DOI: 10.1017/9781009436908

First published online: January 2024

D. J. Hopkins

San Diego State University

Author for correspondence: D. J. Hopkins, dhopkins@sdsu.edu

ABSTRACT: This Element focuses on Sleep No More, a theatre adaptation of Macbeth produced by the British company Punchdrunk. This Element frames the Shakespeare adaptation as part of a system of ghostly citationality through which audiences understand the significance of the past in performances today. Hopkins introduces the concept of "uncanny spectatorship" to describe audience practice in Sleep No More and other performance contexts. The Element positions experiences like Sleep No More as forms of critical inquiry, and, despite its seemingly analog format, Sleep No More is discussed as a valuable site for media research. Ultimately, Sleep No More *and the Discourses of Shakespeare Performance* offers an opportunity to explore a set of concepts that are significant to the subject of Shakespeare Performance and to consider the ways in which audiences interact with bodies, spaces, text, and media.

KEYWORDS: Shakespeare, performance, adaptation, immersive, media

© D. J. Hopkins 2024

ISBNs: 9781009436892 (PB), 9781009436908 (OC)
ISSNs: 2516-0117 (online), 2516-0109 (print)

Contents

Introduction: Adaptation, Remediation, and Ghosts

In this Element, I explore the ways in which a key example of Shakespeare Performance is exemplary of long-standing conversations in the scholarship surrounding Shakespeare's plays. I'll also show how this live immersive experience is surreptitiously in dialogue with media structures. And I'll spend a lot of time talking about ghosts.

Sleep No More is a dance theatre adaptation of *Macbeth*, with many of the plot points and characters of Shakespeare's tragedy distributed over a hundred thousand square feet of renovated warehouse space. *Sleep No More* is produced by Punchdrunk, a London-based company that has become internationally famous for its immersive theatre productions. *Sleep No More* was directed by Punchdrunk founder and Artistic Director Felix Barrett, with choreography by codirector Maxine Doyle. *Sleep No More* premiered in New York City in March 2011, following earlier productions in London and Boston. At the time of publication, Punchdrunk has announced that *Sleep No More* will be closing in February 2024. The venue for *Sleep No More* has been designed to resemble a hotel from the 1930s. Part of one floor looks like the high street of a small Scottish village. And in other parts of the sprawling performance complex, audience members can find a variety of environments that seem straight out of the supernatural settings of Edgar Allan Poe or H. P. Lovecraft. I like to compare *Sleep No More* to a *Macbeth*-themed haunted house.[1] There's nowhere for you to sit in a haunted house, and you keep moving to experience each "performance" until you reach the exit. Comparing *Sleep No More* to a haunted house is more than a bit reductive, though Amy Cook interjects that the comparison is apt, because a haunted house emphasizes "experience over *meaning*." Cook playfully prioritizes a sense of fun over the significance associated with dramatic literature.[2] Still, I don't want to minimize the sophistication of *Sleep No More*, from the vision for this production, to the artistry of its design, to the directing and choreography; further, the performances by the many actors and dancers who

---

[1] See Hopkins, "A Concise Introduction to Immersive Theatre." Portions of the following first appeared in Hopkins, review of *Sleep No More*, 2012.

[2] Personal correspondence (January 3, 2023), original emphasis.

have cycled through the cast are accomplished – often virtuosic. All these achievements have made *Sleep No More* a critically acclaimed production, the object of a lively fandom, a profitable source of revenue for Punchdrunk, and, I argue, a production that is itself historically significant.

Shakespeare Performance is an ideal field for an exploration of the intersection of theatre and media, because the history of Shakespeare is an archive of what has been done with bodies, spaces, and technology over the past four hundred years.[3] The case study here is *Sleep No More*, now internationally recognized as the iconic example of immersive theatre. *Sleep No More* is also a valuable example of Shakespeare Performance because it offers an opportunity to consider what audiences do with bodies, spaces, and technology in the twenty-first century. Admittedly, *Sleep No More* is not an obvious subject for research into the intersection of theatre and new media – here is a performance that appears to be entirely analog and committed to in-real-life experiences. But *Sleep No More* is valuable not only for investigations of Shakespeare in performance and Shakespeare adaptation: despite being devoid of projected images or digital gadgetry of any kind, *Sleep No More* is a productive site for media research. By considering *Sleep No More* in relation to key conversations that frequently surface in the discourses of Shakespeare Performance, I position this particular performance as a form of critical inquiry, one that has held the attention of audiences, scholars, and theatre makers alike because it asks questions both of a history of Shakespeare Performance and of our contemporary culture – and perhaps even offers some answers. *Sleep No More* not only provides new perspectives on a familiar Shakespearean text, but – even more important – it offers revelations about our world and ourselves.

---

[3] The history of Shakespeare Performance can be described as both an archive and a repertoire. Diana Taylor established this distinction as a discourse in the fields of Performance and Theatre Studies. See Taylor, *The Archive and the Repertoire*. It is important to note, though, that "the apparent fixity of the archive tends to incorporate elements of the unstable, of performance." See Hopkins, "Reconsidering the Boredom of King James," p. 481.

What is Shakespeare Performance? I use the phrase "Shakespeare Performance" throughout this Element, and even in its title, to refer to both a history of the *performing* of Shakespeare's plays as well as to the ideas about how Shakespeare's plays should be performed. This phrase implies a long history and a broad range of thought about how Shakespeare has been could be interpreted and realized for audiences – on stage and across multiple media. My disciplinary background is in Theatre Studies, so when I talk about Shakespeare I'm often thinking about "that slippery entity called performance, wherein a Shakespearean text is made flesh by theatrical representation."[4] And that subject is "slippery" because a performance of a play by Shakespeare will mean different things to different audience members; and, as well, each production of Shakespeare may have a different value to different scholars of Shakespeare and performance. W. B. Worthen uses the phrase "Shakespeare Performance Studies" to describe the scholarship of theatrical productions of the plays of Shakespeare. Worthen notes that when Shakespeare scholarship has turned to performance, it has often concentrated on a specific production's relationship to the source text, specifically "the ways that the text's incipient meanings can be framed to address a contemporary audience."[5] Often this text-based analysis relies on a reader's assumptions that lead to the expectation that a performance will simply realize ideas that the reader has identified when reading the source text. By contrast, the scholarship associated with Shakespeare Performance Studies has placed a premium on "the significance of stage performance," a perspective that locates Shakespeare as one element among many in the making of theatre.[6] Taking a performance seriously as a site for the production of Shakespearean knowledge – what a play is *about* – unsettles "expectations of singular meanings" that might derive from a more text-based approach to Shakespeare in the theatre.[7] By Worthen's measure, this Element fits the description of Shakespeare Performance Studies: a work of scholarship about Shakespeare in performance. In this Element, though, I use the phrase

---

[4] Bulman, "Introduction," p. 1.

[5] Worthen, *Shakespeare Performance Studies*, p. 18.

[6] Worthen, *Shakespeare Performance Studies*, p. 18.

[7] Barbara Hodgdon, Shakespeare, Performance, and the Archive, p. 6.

"Shakespeare Performance" to include creative activity – performances, films, and their makers – among the many sources that produce meaning with and through Shakespeare. In short, Shakespeare Performance includes a history of theatrical thought and stage practices that spans centuries and includes multiple media.[8]

Sleep No More occupies a significant place in the history of twenty-first-century Shakespeare Performance because it deploys its source material in the context of an emergent mode of performance – immersive theatre. And it is in good company: Shakespeare has been invoked for centuries to authorize new performance forms and to legitimize new media, from early film to virtual reality (VR). James Bulman has observed that new approaches to performing Shakespeare "have gained an authority once accorded only to the text; new modes of adaptation . . . have fundamentally altered the relationship between actors and audience; and the concept of 'live' performance has been profoundly altered by the digital revolution."[9] But Bulman notes a confounding corollary to these new developments: some examples of contemporary theatre raise the question of "how Shakespeare acquires meaning in performance"; or, to put it another way: "Wherein lies the 'Shakespeareness' of a performance in which the text is marginalized?"[10] This Element leans into that question, encouraging readers to think about *Sleep No More* as a laboratory space in which Shakespeare is deployed as a tool for understanding our embodied, mediatized world. Audiences entering this space are in dialogue with the influence of seemingly absent media as well as the shaping significance of Shakespeare's tragedy *Macbeth*, despite an absence of much of what we associate with Shakespeare: his words.

I've been to this movie before. In my article "Hamlet's Mirror Image," I consider the 2007 production of Shakespeare's *Hamlet* by the venerable

---

[8] This approach is aligned with what Tracy Davis and Peter Marx call a "Critical Media History." Davis and Marx argue that "theatre / performance historiography needs to be understood within an evolving media history," and in Sleep No More *and the Discourses of Shakespeare Performance*, I contribute to the project of locating Shakespeare in that same intermedial creative-critical discourse. See Davis and Marx, "Introduction," p. 3.

[9] Bulman, "Introduction," p. 1. [10] Bulman, "Introduction," p. 3.

experimental theatre company the Wooster Group.[11] That article explores the "relationship between cinematic representation and theatrical performance," focusing on a single representative example of multimedia theatre, buttressed by reference to two films that go out of their way to establish relationships to what Barbara Hodgdon calls "a theatrical-cinematic citational past."[12] I conclude that these and other Shakespeare adaptations (theatrical, cinematic, and otherwise) are part of "a Shakespearean hauntology, a system of ghostly citationality through which we try to understand the significance of the past in present-day performances."[13] Here, I continue the intermedial theatre research begun in that previous study, augmenting and extending that work while introducing new perspectives on Shakespearean performances that blur the (already permeable) boundary between live and media experiences. Greg Giesekam sees "border disputes" along the media/performance boundary as "ironic, given that these media themselves originally borrowed considerably from theatre"; over the last 120 years and more, "each medium has remediated one or more of the others."[14] The value of Shakespeare as a long-standing site for media and performance experimentation is what renders the Wooster Group's production of *Hamlet* a kind of "theatrical-cinematic" ghost story that both is and is not a production of *Hamlet*.[15]

In considering that production of *Hamlet*, Peter Holland wonders "which are the ghosts," the actors on stage or those on screen?[16] The question is apt, but it also feels limited: Shakespeare, too, is ghosted in the

---

[11] See Hopkins, "Hamlet's Mirror Image," p. 15, for films and theatrical productions that "appropriate Shakespeare's mimesis-disrupting strategies both to fetishize and to subvert the conventions of cinema."

[12] Hopkins, "Hamlet's Mirror Image," p. 8; Hodgdon, "Re-Incarnations," p. 204. Hodgdon uses the phrase "a theatrical-cinematic citational past" to refer to Michael Almereyda's 2000 film version of *Hamlet*. The phrase remains valuable with reference to other Shakespeare performances that explicitly locate themselves in relation to a history of Shakespeare performance on stage and screen, including *Sleep No More*.

[13] Hopkins, "Hamlet's Mirror Image," p. 21.

[14] Giesekam, *Staging the Screen*, p. 5. [15] Hodgdon, "Re-Incarnations," p. 204.

[16] Holland, "Haunting Shakespeare," p. 211.

Wooster Group's *Hamlet*. This usage of ghosting is a critical perspective that sees in live theatre a range of performance practices that direct attention to that which seems to be absent. One of the most cited voices in this discourse is Marvin Carlson, whose book *The Haunted Stage: The Theatre as Memory Machine* (2001) not only looks at historical performances through the lens of theatrical ghosting but also considers contemporary performance, with special attention to the Wooster Group.[17] Simply put, theatrical ghosting is a way of looking at theatre that invites the viewer to see what isn't there – whatever that may be will vary, based on the viewer; or on the scholar directing a reader's attention. In the case of the Wooster Group's *Hamlet*, as the audience's attention is pulled back and forth between watching a production of *Hamlet* and (at the same time) watching a film version of *Hamlet*, the idea of the Shakespearean appears, disappears, and reappears, much like the celluloid specter of the actor Richard Burton, projected on the upstage screen.[18] But theatrical ghosting is not only found somewhere between a live performance and a mediated one. Holland himself expands the concept when he invites consideration of another haunted site: "the one place for ghosts that has least often been considered in work on ghosts in the theatre: ghosts in the audience."[19] So, ghosts can be found in lots of places in the theatre: between the performers, in the "contested space" of the dramatic source material and its author function, and among the audience members – the very people who are busily receiving and interpreting a complex theatrical event. Such a fluid conception of ghosting demands a more dynamic critical approach. Holland's inquiry needs to be spatialized. The question is not *which* are the ghosts, but *where* are the ghosts? Answering that question will require a kind of "uncanny spectatorship": an audience who can see ghosts. I'll talk about

---

[17] Carlson, *The Haunted Stage*. For Carlson on The Wooster Group, see pp. 168–172.

[18] Rebecca Schneider supplements theories of performance as "vanishment" by adding that performance is also defined by "re-appearance": "like so many ghosts at the door marked 'disappeared.'" Schneider, *Performing Remains*, p. 102.

[19] Holland, "Haunting Shakespeare," p. 212, and see pp. 211–15.

various forms of theatrical ghosts throughout this Element, gradually developing what uncanny spectatorship looks like in practice.

My *Sleep No More* research engages with that of other scholars who have framed Shakespeare's plays as dynamic resources, as raw material for new performances and new experiences. The principle that I adopt as foundational to my approach to Shakespeare is that performances, games, and classrooms – among other sites – can be alternative places to locate Shakespearean authority and the production of knowledge. Why is that important? I think that many people, including many scholars, still see "Shakespeare" as *writing*, as *book space* determined solely by literary conceptions that frame Shakespeare as a cultural icon, rendering his plays as inert relics. Sleep No More *and the Discourses of Shakespeare Performance* joins a chorus of voices that seek to disrupt the purely literary conceptions that have accreted around Shakespeare. That's why I often write "Shakespeares" as plural: to emphasize the multiplicity and fluidity of Shakespeare as a field of scholarly study and as the subject of cultural and creative production.

Shakespeare Performance has always been a site for more than just the explication of Shakespeare's texts. Shakespeare's plays in performance are "strange tools," in Alva Noë's evocative phrase. Noë writes: "A work of art is a strange tool, an alien implement. We make strange tools to investigate ourselves."[20] Shakespeare Performance is no exception to Noë's rule – indeed, it may be an exemplar. As Worthen has forcefully argued, Shakespeare can and should be seen as a tool for exploring theatre and performance more generally. Worthen's call has been taken up by Susan Bennett, among other scholars, and it can be expanded further. A remark by my colleague Eric Smigel has served for years as a motto for my research and teaching: "Art is a mode of critical inquiry." Nick Salvato comes to a similar conclusion when writing about theatre productions that frame performance more like a scholarly argument *about* a play than supposedly transparent productions *of* a play.[21] These critical perspectives run contrary

---

[20] Noë, *Strange Tools*, p. 30.

[21] See Salvato, "Uncloseting Drama," p. 36: "The Wooster Group's approach constitutes a mode of analysis more akin to the work of literary criticism than it is to the goals of traditional dramaturgy."

to many literary inquiries into Shakespeare Performance; these often ask what stable information *about* Shakespeare we can learn *from* a given performance. By contrast, I frame Shakespeare as a (strange) tool for critical inquiry, not only its object. And so, the question becomes: what new knowledges can audiences learn *with* Shakespeare *through* performance?

This Element brings together studies in Shakespeare Performance and immersive theatre, an approach that centers the role of theatre space in constructing audience experience at *Sleep No More*. Kim Solga frames performance space as "an independent but also an *interdependent* function of theatrical composition." Writing about the reconstructed Globe in London, a significant Shakespearean site, Solga concludes that it offers "a lesson in shared human spacing, a way of orienting us toward space as collectively embodied: made, and re-made, together."[22] In this Element, I describe *Sleep No More* as another site where theatrical performance is interdependent with Shakespearean textuality, audience experience, and media forms.

While other scholarship has considered aspects of *Sleep No More*, I will provide both a comprehensive introduction to this influential example of immersive theatre and also take the reader on a deep dive into the critical conversations about Shakespeare Performance that *Sleep No More* "engages and complicates."[23] Though I focus on a single case study, I develop an argument that begins with encountering *Sleep No More*, trying to reckon with what the audience does at this immersive performance, and turns to thinking about its origins and history. Then, I open up a discussion of *Sleep No More* as an example of Shakespeare adaptation. Adaptation relies on revision; and the ideal audience member of a theatrical adaptation is one who can recognize (and even enjoy) the differences between a source and the new, revised production. For me, thinking about adaptation leads directly to thoughts of *theatrical ghosting*. Theatrical ghosting is a critical practice in Theatre Studies that invites audiences to see what *isn't there* in

---

[22] Solga, *Theory for Theatre Studies*, pp. 1, 53 (original emphasis).

[23] Thanks to the anonymous reader of this Element manuscript whose warm response included this evocative phrase.

performance (as well as what's right in front of their eyes). *Sleep No More* is a performance environment optimized for exploration via the perspectives of theatrical ghosting, and the various kinds of (critical) ghosts that one may find in the (spooky) environment of *Sleep No More* is a central concern of this Element. And speaking of seeing things that aren't there, film and other media are never seen in *Sleep No More*, and yet references to specific films and the very idea of cinema are important to this production. Shakespeare scholarship frequently considers the place of film and other media in Shakespeare performance. So I discuss the ways that film surfaces in *Sleep No More*, with particular attention to the way it relies on *remediation*, a media studies concept that has a surprising force in this seemingly media-free performance. Alongside these engagements, I unpack a few other key concepts, including the gamification of theatre and the quarrelsome scholarship of Shakespeare's plays in performance. A throughline develops throughout Sleep No More *and the Discourses of Shakespeare Performance* and unifies these explorations of current thinking about the performance of Shakespeare's plays: a consideration of audience experience. Immersive theatre makes the practices of *audience-ing* explicit; and the absent presence of Shakespeare in *Sleep No More* calls for deeper consideration of how spectatorship works in this immersive adaptation.

Ultimately, this Element demonstrates that *Sleep No More* is not an outlier among performances of Shakespeare. Contrary to some dismissive reviews and retrograde critiques, *Sleep No More* is not an exception among examples of Shakespeare Performance, it is exemplary. In fact, *Sleep No More* is representative of the ideas and discourses that shape the scholarship of Shakespeare Performance Studies.

What Is *Sleep No More* . . . ?

For those unfamiliar with *Sleep No More*, some background is warranted. I'll follow with adeep dive into the scholarly discourses that are provoked by this example of Shakespearean theatre, and then jump to adiscussion of the ways in which *Sleep No More*, though lacking multimedia elements or visible gadgetry, is nevertheless amedia-saturated performance environment.

Audience members to *Sleep No More* arrive at an unmarked warehouse in the Meatpacking District of New York City. A small brass plaque on the brick wall that reads "The McKittrick Hotel" is the only indication that attendees are in the right place – that and the line of other attendees waiting outside a black steel door. On one occasion, I arrived just after 6:30 p.m. for a 7 p.m. entry time, hoping to be in the first group taken into the performance at 7:30 p.m. The order of entry is determined by playing cards distributed to audience members at "reception" (the hotel-themed term for the *Sleep No More* box office). I was handed a deuce; apparently, I was just a few minutes too late to get an ace, which would mean that I'd be in the first group to enter. When I lightly shared my disappointment, the guy working the reception desk playfully told me that his last name was Hopkins, too. "So, I'll give you this instead," he said, pulling a card out of his shirt pocket and handing me an ace of spades. I smiled and said, "Thank you so much, um, *Mr. Hopkins*." It seemed a polite little joke, and I was already getting into the interactive spirit – why else would the box office staff keep spare aces in their pockets? He replied, obviously enjoying our little scene: "You're welcome ... *Mr. Hopkins*. Enjoy your stay at The McKittrick."

After collecting a playing card at reception, audience members enter *Sleep No More* through a dark hallway with several sharp turns. Punchdrunk's in-house lingo calls an entry like this a "decompression maze": a disorienting but nonthreatening passage from the ordinary world of box office and coat check to the border region of *Sleep No More*'s narrative world.[24] By "nonthreatening," I mean that no one is going to jump at you from behind a corner, haunted-house style. Some first-time visitors are afraid that they will encounter a cat-scare in the maze; on one occasion, I reassured a fellow audience member who was hesitant to enter the dark hallway just beyond the box office. But a Punchdrunk decompression maze is more like a mindfulness exercise: the activity of negotiating an unfamiliar space in the dark gives audience members the space and time to transition out of the real world (physically as well as cognitively)

---

[24] For "decompression maze," see Shendruk, "An Industry Built on the Suspension of Disbelief."

and into a narrative space in which disorientation is part of the pleasure of the experience.

Audience members emerge from the darkness of the decompression maze into the brightness and noise of the Manderley, the cabaret of the McKittrick Hotel – which is not a real hotel, though the fake hotel does have a real bar. Audience members are welcomed to the 1930s by in-character hosts wearing period attire. The audience members can order drinks and chat freely in the Manderley while they wait to be called to enter the performance itself. But the Manderley location is more than just a bar, more than just the lobby of *Sleep No More*: for attendees who are willing to start a conversation, the characters in the bar know things about the characters elsewhere in the explicitly narrative locations of the McKittrick. So, despite the cash transactions, the chat over drinks, and the kinda corny convention of costumed hosts, audience members entering the Manderley have already slipped into the space of *Sleep No More*.

Before entering the performance space itself, audience members are taken to a small room adjacent to the Manderley, where all are given white masks that resemble traditional Venetian carnival masks (Figure 1). At this point, a costumed performer from the Manderley admonishes all audience members to remain silent throughout the performance and to keep their masks on at all times. All of Punchdrunk's large-scale productions have used a variation of this device, and the company insists that the masks make a profound contribution to the overall theatrical experience. Functionally, the masks distinguish audience members from performers.[25] The performative functions of the masks used in Punchdrunk performances are much debated. W. B. Worthen argues that the masks reestablish proscenium-like values that disrupt the apparent immersivity of the performance and autonomy of the audience.[26] As a significant feature of the theatrical event, the masks render the audience of *Sleep No More* both a part of the scenography and a ghostly chorus witnessing the action alongside the characters.

---

[25] Freshwater, *Theatre & Audience*, p. 66.
[26] Worthen, *Shakespeare Performance*, pp. 142–44.

Figure 1 Macbeth and Lady Macbeth with masked audience members. Photo: Robin Roemer for The McKittrick Hotel.

The audience is taken in small groups into the multistory performance space, usually via elevator, and released to wander at will through what may seem like a warren of spooky installation art. These spaces include a hospital with rows of empty beds, adjacent to another institutional room full of 1930s-era bathtubs; these two rooms, which make a kind of sense together, surreally adjoin a foggy maze of sticks that leads past a taxidermied ram to a little wooden hut with a locked door. Audience members can peek between the slats of its walls, as I did, peering into the hut's Cornell box-like interior. Another part of the *Sleep No More* performance space resembles a row of deserted shops, like the high street of a Scottish village. Each shop is dense with 1930s details: furniture, photos, and – for those who care to spend time going through file cabinets and desk drawers – correspondence between the characters. One shop is a candy store, Paisley Sweets; jars of old-fashioned sweets are on display, and audience members can sample them. On my first visit to *Sleep No More*, I found an account book under the counter of the candy store, beautifully bound in period materials. While I was leafing through this obsessively created prop, a scrap of paper fell to the counter: on it were written the words, "Blood will have blood." I left the creepy little piece of paper there for someone else to discover. Many audience members spend time exploring such details, but early in my first visit, I was eager to find live performers in the sprawling theatre space.

Though unified by the idea of a hotel, the *Sleep No More* performance space is highly eclectic. The (initially disorienting) multistory venue is referred to as The McKittrick Hotel, a fictional location the name of which is taken from Hitchcock's film *Vertigo*. Hitchcock is one of the guiding spirits of this production, which merges the supernatural darkness of *Macbeth* with the suspenseful atmosphere of *Vertigo*, *Rebecca*, and other Hitchcock films. When encountered alone, many *Sleep No More* actors perform actions based on a vaguely Hitchcockian reimagining of a Shakespearean character – Malcolm is reimagined as an obsessive private investigator, to take one example (Figure 2). Sequences involving multiple characters offer choreographic evocations of scenes from *Macbeth* or silent exchanges that might have occurred between the acts of Shakespeare's tragedy. One landmark scene early in the performance takes place in Hecate's "Dead Bar," an eerie saloon where Macbeth meets the witches for a demonic dance party. This orgiastic rave is accompanied by a thumping, anachronistic techno soundtrack – music at odds with the Hitchcock scores and 1930s-era songs heard elsewhere in the McKittrick. As the rave ends, actors and audience gradually disperse. One witch lingers until most of the audience leaves, at which point she performs a virtuosic dance solo along the bar at the far side of the room (under the watchful gaze of Hecate), before she, too, runs off and disappears in the dark corridors (Figure 3).

Along with the masks worn by the audience, music is an essential feature of the *Sleep No More* experience. Bernard Herrmann's scores to Hitchcock films are sampled frequently. The soundtrack plays from hidden speakers, rising to a climax at just the right time and in just the right place as characters meet, collide, and dance. Sound is not uniform throughout *Sleep No More*. The *Sleep No More* superfans who publish as paisleysweets have compiled an obsessively detailed documentation of the

Figure 2 Malcolm with masked audience members. Photo: Yaniv Schulman for The McKittrick Hotel.

Figure 3 Hecate and one of the witches. Photo: Alick Crossley for The McKittrick Hotel.

songs and tracks that can be heard throughout the sprawling performance complex at different times and places, including noting the narrative moments supported by the music.[27] *Sleep No More*'s sound design is an achievement, demonstrating the stagecraft and narrative control behind a seemingly anarchic production in a large, multilevel space. Often, though, the sound design has a reductive side effect: music structures several scenes in ways that reduce character interaction to melodrama formulations. In one case, a pregnant Lady Macduff runs across the hotel lobby carrying an overcoat and a suitcase; she is confronted by a male character whose menace is forcefully illustrated by Herrmann's music. A risky dance sequence follows, conveying the aggression of their confrontation: Lady Macduff is slammed into furniture and spun toward audience members, who have to hustle to get out of the way. At the end of this duet, Lady Macduff is abandoned on the floor; Macbeth exits, and a few moments later, her husband races in. The music swells as Macduff cradles his unresponsive wife before he collapses onto a sofa. He exits alone with great remorse, as the treacly soundtrack informs us. Then, with a change in music, Lady Macduff rises. Is this a different scene? Is there a logical explanation for her recovery, or is this another example of the surreal theatricality that permeates *Sleep No More*? Regardless, she collects her coat and suitcase, and leaves.

Not every interaction is so schematic. One of *Sleep No More*'s most well-known scenes focuses on the Macbeths in their bedroom: the king and queen perform in and around a claw-footed bathtub filled with bloody water. She bathes him; they argue wordlessly, but with a lot of shouting and sexy-aggressive dance and expressive gestures; they change their clothes; they dance again on the bed; then Macbeth heads off to commit murder (Figure 4). Left alone, Lady Macbeth has a solo on the bed while mumbling the only words that most audience-participants are likely to hear all night: "Out, damn spot," whispered over and over as she hurls herself at the mattress and padded walls in choreographic self-harm, an example of what Maurizio Calbi might call "the spectral remainder of language" in Shakespeare Performance.[28]

---

[27] *Paisleysweets, "All There Is," January 26, 2013.*

[28] Calbi, *Spectral Shakespeares*, p. 144.

Figure 4 Macbeth and Lady Macbeth. Photo: Yaniv Schulman.

That first time I attended *Sleep No More*, I exited the candy shop when I saw a character in a 1930s-era dress walk by the large, plate-glass window. I joined a small clutch of audience members, and we followed her along the Scottish street on the fourth floor; she entered another shop, and I watched as she hastily took scissors to a black-and-white photo and placed the cutout in a locket. When the performer finished her mysterious craft project, she took the hand of an audience member and drew him into an adjoining room, closing the door behind them. Another audience member tried the doorknob and found it locked. Facing a (narrative) dead end, we turned and left. Encounters such as these flesh out the McKittrick's narrative as much as Shakespeare's, expanding this fictional site's "constructed history."[29]

---

[29] Masters, "Site and Seduction," p. 21.

As Amy Cook observes, "character here does not line up neatly with Shakespeare's literary text."[30] In fact Shakespeare's text is supplemented with other texts: some *Sleep No More* characters are adapted from Hitchcockian sources or are entirely invented. Sequences involving multiple characters offer choreographic evocations of scenes from *Macbeth* or silent exchanges that might have occurred between the acts of Shakespeare's tragedy. Another of *Sleep No More*'s most memorable scenes is a banquet that crowds most of the main characters at a table in the hotel's grand ballroom (and crowds a good deal of the audience on the dance floor to watch) (Figure 5). Staged as a slow-motion nightmare, with moody contemporary music drawn from David Lynch's 1997 film *Lost Highway*, the scene focuses on the guilt and lust of Macbeth and Lady Macbeth, who are joined at the table by some of their entourage (Banquo, of course, makes an entrance) and the witches (Figure 6). This banquet is performed at the end of each "loop" of the three-hour performance.

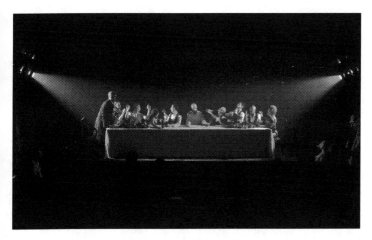

Figure 5 The banquet scene. Photo: Lucas Jackson, REUTERS / Alamy Stock Photo.

---

[30] Cook, *Building Character*, p. 117.

Figure 6 The Ghost of Banquo at the banquet. Photo: Umi Akiyoshi for The McKittrick Hotel.

I wandered the rooms and installations for about half an hour, that first time at *Sleep No More*, before I saw my first performer. Some time later, I found myself sprinting through dim corridors along with other audience members, chasing the title character. Losing him in what appeared at the time to be a theatrical maze, I found myself wondering, "Where is Macbeth?" One might just as well ask, "Where is *Macbeth*?" Because if you're looking for actors delivering lines from the Scottish Play, you're in the wrong place. Amy Cook responds that the "frustrated search for Macbeth in *Sleep No More*" should prompt a reconsideration of "the 'location' of a character."[31] It's a point worth noting, because *Macbeth* (like its title character) is everywhere and nowhere in *Sleep No More*.

The Illegibility of Immersive Theatre

Sleep No More offers an expansive investigation of the play whose words it largely eschews. Scenes such as those I have described provide engaging

---

[31] Cook, *Building Character*, p. 117.

explorations of *Macbeth*'s tragic landscape. Some of those who attend *Sleep No More*, though, find that landscape and its elusive characters incomprehensible – or perhaps a better word would be *illegible*. A number of reviews in popular periodicals have dismissed *Sleep No More* specifically because of its wordlessness, revealing a literary bias in their theatre expectations (and implying that a wordless performance of a play by Shakespeare is simply not Shakespeare at all), while other reviews dismiss *Sleep No More*'s use of space as a gimmick or oddity. The assessment of *Sleep No More* by Ben Brantley in the *New York Times* exemplifies such sentiments. Regarding this Shakespeare adaptation, Brantley concludes, dismissively: "this is not the place to look for insights into Shakespeare" (as if providing "insights into Shakespeare" were the unambiguous raison d'être for the performance of Shakespeare). But this casual dismissal is among the most substantial claims in Brantley's review, which includes several petty quips. Brantley negligently describes Punchdrunk as a "site-specific theatre company," a phrase that gives him license to describe *Sleep No More* as no more than "an adventure in décor." He kicks this joke later, dismissing *Sleep No More* as unable to access the "interior worlds" of its characters, emphasizing instead "the World of Interiors." Brantley is entertained by the "comely," "lissome," and "lithe" bodies in "this chic spook house," but he finds no intellectual substance in *Sleep No More*, to the point that he explicitly refrains from conceding any relationship to Shakespeare or *Macbeth*. Instead of a "place to look for insights into Shakespeare," Brantley finds only a voyeuristic "sense of guilty enjoyment, translated into theatrical terms."[32]

Hilton Als, too, finds in *Sleep No More* an emphasis on surfaces. For Als, writing in the *New Yorker*, the production produces not intellectual engagement but "an over-all emotional effect, in which décor and dance are equal to the dramaturgy." Readers of his reviews may well expect Als to prefer word-rich stagings of dramatic literature. Als is troubled, it seems, to have gone to the theatre expecting someone to read Shakespeare's *Macbeth* to him, only to find instead so much dance: "We cannot connect with the characters through the thing that we share: language. We can only watch as

---

[32] Brantley, "Shakespeare Slept Here."

the performers reduce theatre to its rudiments: bodies moving in space."
One doesn't need to be a linguist or philosopher to observe that language is
not something "we" share unambiguously, nor a dance scholar or choreographer to observe that the movement of bodies in space is in fact "a thing
that we share" as well. But Als doesn't agree: the piece, "stripped of what we
usually expect of a theatrical performance," ceases to be theatre for him.
Instead, Als argues that it is "anxiety that keeps us moving from floor to
floor and room to room, like shuddering inmates." I disagree, but it's
a beautiful phrase, one in which i can see that Als perceives himself as
part of the performance – one of the "shuddering inmates" of this asylum-
like hotel – rather than an external observer of it. Such a degree of
participation is a fundamental premise of immersive theatre. Als acknowledges that he is present for the performance, and he's experiencing it, he's
just also rejecting it. For while Als, too, "didn't feel that the Bard was the
central dramaturgical impulse here" (as we might expect from anyone
unironically calling Shakespeare "the Bard"), he did appreciate other
aspects of his *Sleep No More* experience. Describing himself sitting in the
Manderley Bar, Als concludes by noting his struggle to assemble his
experience of *Sleep No More* as a whole: "Does this mean that, if one forgets
moments of the piece in this doomed party atmosphere, it's superficial? Yes.
Does this mean that the profound role the piece plays in altering one's
consciousness makes it a deep work, too? Yes." Unlike Brantley, Als can
assess the production despite its divergence from his preferred forms of
theatre. Als admires aspects of *Sleep No More*, particularly the music and
sound design (a "dreadful, perfect soundtrack") and sections of the scenic
design and installation art (though here again belittled as "décor"), but he
needs language in order for *Sleep No More* to be a fully satisfying theatre
experience. Thus, his favorable concessions aside, Als is resistant to seeing
Sleep No More as "theatrical performance," which leaves him unable to
perceive the immersive aspect of the production as anything other than
a decorative corollary to the emotional content of its "shadowy, mannered,
morally terrible" world.[33] Any depth that Als finds in *Sleep No More* is,
paradoxically, on the surface.

[33] Als, "Shadow and Act."

I dwell on these journalistic reviews to illustrate a widespread phenomenon: established critics of major US publications are so unfamiliar with immersive performance that they don't know how to write about it.[34] Josephine Mâchon has described this kind of reaction to immersive performance: "The implication in these responses is that there is a dislike of work that is not driven by linear narrative; that there is a resistance to the perceived 'onus on us' to both create and enjoy the work"; and that audience participation in immersive performance's is "humiliating in practice and inconsequential in effect." As she observes, reviewers critical of immersive performance argue that "it cannot compare to the clarity and complexity of ideas expressed through the written play."[35] Of course, despite such negative reviews, droves of audience members attend immersive shows, and a number of popular writers review the form favorably. Lyn Gardner, a London-based theatre writer, argues that "Punchdrunk shows require you to work at them and that is not a bad thing; to make demands upon an audience."[36] Brantley sees himself as an active audience member, too, but his view of the relationship between audience and performance and the demands that one makes on the other is clearly distinct from that of Gardner.[37]

Comprehending immersive performance proves a challenge for many, including those theatre critics and writers whose previous theatregoing has focused on realism, frontally aligned proscenium productions, and linear narratives. With ingrained expectations formed from dramatic literature, some mainstream theatre writers find that performances that deviate from those expectations are, to one degree or another, illegible. Matt Wolf's *New York Times* review of the most recent Punchdrunk production, *The Burnt City* (2022), begins with a welcome acknowledgment of how immersive theatre works: "It's unusual in a live performance to construct your

---

[34] There are exceptions. See Helen Shaw's "The Wild Invention of *Fefu and Her Friends*." Lyn Gardner was an early champion of Punchdrunk. See Gardner, "Immersive Theatre & Performance."

[35] Mâchon, *Immersive Theatres*, p. 41.

[36] Quoted in Mâchon, *The Punchdrunk Encyclopaedia*, p. 122.

[37] See Brantley, "Why I'll Never Stop."

own narrative, shaping the event as you see fit. But that has long been part of the appeal of Punchdrunk, the ambitious immersive theater company."[38] Notably, neither of the lead theatre reviewers covered this latest Punchdrunk production for the *Times*, despite the indisputable international visibility of *Burnt City*.

From reading a number of reviews of *Sleep No More*, I conclude that many authors of these reviews, otherwise accomplished theatregoers, attended only one performance – as they might any other show – with predictably limited perspectives on a production that cannot be fully absorbed after one performance, or even two or three. Why bother talking about the inability of a few journalistic theatre critics to write about immersive theatre? These reviews and reviewers are representative of popular perspectives: a resistance to immersive theatre as a form and, in the case of *Sleep No More*, a corresponding resistance to radical adaptations of Shakespeare. These reviews make clear that even experienced theatre writers often can't see what they can't see. In these examples, the authors want a performance that is right there in front of them in its entirety all the time, as in the proscenium spaces where they developed their theatre-watching habits. I've taken time to analyze the inadequacy of these reviews to demonstrate the need for another way of *audience-ing* and another way of writing about immersive theatre.

Still, Brantley's complaint about *Sleep No More* echoes in my mind: "this is not the place to look for insights into Shakespeare." His dismissive remark raises a valuable question: If *Sleep No More* isn't the place to look for insights into Shakespeare, then what is it a place *for* . . . ?

Making Meaning with the Audiences of Immersive Theatre

I've seen multiple performances of Punchdrunk's *Sleep No More* in two locations: at the long-running McKittrick Hotel location in New York City, and at The McKinnon Hotel, the satellite production of *Sleep No More* seven thousand miles away in Shanghai, China. The durable international interest in *Sleep No More* depends on its obsessively dense design elements; the

[38] Wolf, "The Carnage of War."

creative, physically demanding choreography; and a louche world made possible by an inventive appropriation of Shakespeare's text. But then again, the same could be said about many Shakespeare productions on stage and screen alike. The crucial difference is the attention given by the Punchdrunk team to the role of the audience. Early performances of *Sleep No More* were immediately popular, making it a rarity in the experimental theatre world: an innovative performance that appealed to general audiences as well as to specialist theatregoers.

The production's strategies of audience engagement have made it an exemplar of the immersive theatre form. W. B. Worthen describes the way an audience member of *Sleep No More* gathers information. He begins by outlining a premise that scholars of Punchdrunk's work and immersive performance in general take as a given: that the value of *Sleep No More* stems from the ways in which the performance "seems to resist the frontal, objectivizing epistemology of modern proscenium theatricality" by placing audience members "*in* the event." The result is that the "apparently ... casual performance structure" of *Sleep No More* "multiplies the practice of our performance as spectators."[39] This is a critical premise: *Sleep No More* frames audience members as co-performers who must take action in order to fulfill the performance – or at least to activate their own personal experience of the performance. The immersive epistemology that Worthen provides is a way of knowing that Brantley consciously rejects, one that eludes even the more sympathetic Als. The "process-based spectatorship" of immersive theatre is a challenge to conventional theatre and its spectatorial practices; it is a challenge, too, for some theatregoers, though for others it is an exciting new mode of performance for specialists and general audiences alike.[40]

For my purposes, I want to frame immersive theatre as the extension of a history of long-standing if marginal theatrical practices, not just an emerging trend. Mâchon invites comparison between immersive performance and "religious and cultural" acts of literal immersion in water, acts that carry "transformational implications." Indeed, Mâchon argues that

---

[39] Worthen, *Shakespeare Performance Studies*, pp. 83, 85 (added emphasis).

[40] For "process-based spectatorship," see Dinesh, *Memos from a Theatre Lab*, 122.

"the broad church of physical and visual theatres" employs techniques indebted to "ancient and international rituals and theatre practices."[41] Where Worthen describes an immersive epistemology at work in *Sleep No More*, Mâchon sees in "the broad church" of immersive performance an "interactive exchange of energy and experience" that she describes with the term *praesance*. More phenomenology than epistemology, Mâchon's work explores the emotional and haptic affordances of immersive performance and the corresponding experiences of audiences. For Mâchon, immersive theatre, and Punchdrunk performances in particular, "enhance the live(d) audience-performer-participant" experience of theatregoing.[42] Mâchon uses various terms to describe an attendee of immersive theatre: *audience-participant*, *audience-immersant*, and even *participant-adventurer*.[43] For Mâchon, the audience-participant is "an interactive agent in the performance"; indeed, "the physical insertion and direct participation of the audience member in the work *must* be a vital component and is a defining feature" of immersive performance, particularly that of Punchdrunk.[44] I adopt her term *audience-participant* when discussing the kind of performance that requires "active decision making" from its audience, not merely the intellectually engaged spectator described by Brantley and theorized by Jacques Rancière.[45] Audience engagement at *Sleep No More* becomes especially intense for audience-participants drawn into a "one-on-one" performance. While not unique to Punchdrunk, one-on-ones have become a signature feature of their large-scale immersive productions. Here's my most memorable one-on-one experience . . .

Late in my first visit to Sleep No More, as yet unsure whether the performance would have a conventional ending, I decided to revisit my favorite locations. I found my way back to the maze of sticks, past the taxidermied ram, to the little wooden hut. I peeked inside – a pair of eyes peeked back at me. A ghostly woman in a 1930s-era nurse's uniform promptly exited the hut, took me by the arm, and

[41] Mâchon, *Immersive Theatres*, pp. xiv, 28. [42] Mâchon, *Immersive Theatres*, p. 44.

[43] Mâchon, *Immersive Theatres*, p. 3.

[44] Mâchon, *Immersive Theatres*, p. 57 (original emphasis).

[45] Mâchon, *Immersive Theatres*, p. 28; and see Brantley, "Why I'll Never Stop"; and Rancière, *Emancipated Spectator*, pp. 1–23.

led me back inside. Once we were back in the hut, she seated me in a chair before shuttering the window and locking the door. This non-Shakespearean character, called The Matron, then reached behind my head and took off my mask — a shocking intimacy after two hours of enforced masquerade.[46] *She spooned cold tea into my mouth from a chipped cup, then spoke at length (another shock, to hear an actor's voice): she told me a sinister bedtime story. During this performance, the Matron was never farther away from me than knees-to-knees, and often closer. At the climax of her story, she lifted me out of my chair with her hands pressed on both sides of my head and the tip of her nose pressed against my nose as she shouted: "Blood will have blood!" (That's right, she shouted the very phrase that I'd found earlier on that scrap of paper in the candy shop.) The Matron then recomposed herself, put my mask back on, and shoved me unceremoniously out of her hut.*

One-on-ones like this one are intense, up-close performances and, unlike the rest of *Sleep No More*, they're usually wordy. While it is true that the only words someone is likely to hear a character speak in the course of *Sleep No More* are Lady Macbeth's Shakespearean mutterings, for a lucky few there are spoken performances to be found; one-on-ones often draw on non-Shakespearean, supplementary source material for their text.

Though the hourly looping establishes repetition as a key structure, *Sleep No More* does indeed have a formal ending. Late in the third hour, audience members are gradually shepherded out of each floor and downstairs to the ballroom, where the banquet scene is repeated one last time, with a spectacular, stagey difference: Macbeth climbs up on a chair atop the banquet table, a noose looped round his neck; he steps off as we and the guests attending the banquet watch, his body hanging over the floor of the ballroom. In a final one-on-one-like gesture, Lady Macbeth surreptitiously selects one audience member, and the two walk in formal procession under Macbeth, still gently swinging above, leading the audience back to the Manderley. In a quiet corner of the bar, now bustling with post-show patrons, Lady Macbeth removes the audience-participant's mask and leans in close to whisper, "Welcome back," before disappearing into the crowd.

---

[46] The *Sleep No More* program refers to this character as "Matron Long" and provides a brief biography, p. 17.

As this series of performance anecdotes documents, audience engagement is a defining feature of *Sleep No More*, as it is with other immersive experiences. In fact, audience engagement can be seen to be an organizing structure of this and other Punchdrunk productions. Mâchon defines immersive theatre as a species of performance in which "the audience-participant is imaginatively and sceno-graphically reoriented in another place" as part of a "sensory and participatory" event that occurs "in places outside of traditional theatre venues." Such an immersive environment is, for Mâchon, "*both* a conceptual ... space *and* an inhabited, physical space."[47] This conception of immersive theatre puts me in mind of Shakespeare's famous observation: "All the world's a stage and all the men and women merely players." In the case of immersive theatre, this aphorism often feels rather literal, as distinctions between audience space and performer space are collapsed.[48] What remains is the shared space of immersive theatre, charged with the potential for performance and participation.

Mâchon identifies "a particular kind of audience" that is attracted to – and in turn *produced by* – the "involvement" characteristic of immersive performance. Extending the claims of Susan Bennett's landmark study of theatre audiences, Mâchon argues that "the aesthetic, corporeal, and intel-lectual dimensions of spectatorship in immersive theatre" innovate on theatrical spectatorship more generally. Mâchon recounts seeing herself in a mirror during a performance of Punchdrunk's *The Drowned Man*: "I'm that grainy *ghostly* reflection; a present-absence, absent-presence," conclud-ing that immersive audience-participants are "spectators to our own experience."[49] This audience-as-ghost analogy runs through writing

---

[47] Mâchon, *Immersive Theatres*, pp. 63–64 (original emphasis).

[48] Practices that break down the distance (conceptual as well as physical) between audience space and performance space have been the subject of scholarly consideration for decades, often using the phrase "environmental theatre." For a summary of this discourse, see Hopkins, "A Concise Introduction to Immersive Theatre." For foundational texts, see Aronson, *History and Theory of Environmental Scenography*; and Schechner, "6 Axioms for Environmental Theatre."

[49] Mâchon, "Watching, Attending, Sense-Making," p. 35 (added emphasis); and see Bennett, *Theatre Audiences*.

about Punchdrunk performance. Indeed, Punchdrunk's own in-house lingo reiterates this analogy: as Barrett himself explains, the masks "make the rest of the audience dissolve into generic, *ghostly* presences, so that each person can explore the space alone."[50] To return, then to the question I asked earlier: a spatialized approach to Shakespeare adaptation asks not *which* are the ghosts, but *where* are the ghosts? *Sleep No More* offers one response to that question: among the performers, wearing masks.

The Punchdrunk Encyclopaedia (2019), edited by Mâchon, offers a number of insights (some conflicting) into how the company imagines the use of masks by audiences and their impact on performance. Punchdrunk has evolved mask use over a decade or more, and masking is now seen as an essential "mechanism for participation and presence" in the company's large-scale productions due to the "sense of anonymous immersion" that the masks are thought to confer on the audience-participant. Mâchon argues that through the masks audience-participants are "removed from the traditional role of the passive, hidden audience": "they become part of the scenography and sometimes actually . . . frame the action."[51] Indeed, many photographs of *Sleep No More* feature audience members flanking the performers or framing the space in exactly the kind of scenographic role that Mâchon describes. "The effect is that audience merges with mise-en-scène – *eerily* present witnesses, no longer spectators but *spectres* in the shadows."[52] The ghostly status of the masked audience-participant is paradoxical: removed from the story, but not hidden; insubstantial, but active; ignored by most of the performers, most of the time, but included in the picture as part of the visual life of the production. As a theatrical device, masks contribute to the immersive effect less by what they confer on a masked individual and more by the "ghostly anonymity"

---

[50] F. Barrett, quoted in *Sleep No More* program, p. 24 (added emphasis).
[51] Mâchon, *The Punchdrunk Encyclopaedia*, p. 178. The *Encyclopaedia* is described as "written and prepared by Josephine Mâchon with Punchdrunk" (p. iii). The handsomely designed book straddles the line between reference text and marketing product.
[52] Mâchon, "Watching, Attending, Sense-Making," p. 41 (added emphasis).

they produce when an individual looks around at other audience members.[53]

Mâchon emerged as an early authority on Punchdrunk and has since become the unofficial scholar for the company, as evidenced by the collaborative *Encyclopaedia*. While Mâchon's work is clearly scholarship, it is also clearly partisan. Worthen is rather more skeptical of Punchdrunk's immersive ambitions and the liberatory claims of mask use. Even while Worthen articulates the audience experience of *Sleep No More*, he is laying the groundwork for a critique of Punchdrunk's perspective on Shakespeare and performance. In *Shakespeare Performance Studies*, Worthen provides both praiseful (at times almost awestruck) firsthand accounts of his experiences attending *Sleep No More* alongside incisive critiques of the supposed emancipation of the Punchdrunk spectator. Both Mâchon and Worthen are in dialogue with Rancière. Mâchon compares Punchdrunk's performance practices favorably to Rancière's "emancipated spectator"; Worthen critiques Punchdrunk for its "duplicity," finding not freedom in Punchdrunk's work but an "illusory sense of agency."[54] Worthen discusses Rancière's relevance to *Sleep No More* before concluding with an argument that echoes Brantley's: "we are less the agents of the performance than its furniture." For Worthen, the masks worn by the audience of *Sleep No More* are the strategic approximation of the proscenium: "The mask performs the work of the darkened auditorium and the theatre seat, separating, individualizing, and interiorizing us as a group of spectators."[55] Worthen's perspective is reinforced by *Sleep No More*'s director and Punchdrunk artistic director Felix Barrett: "Handing out the masks is like assigning seats in an auditorium. It establishes each individual as part of an audience, and creates a boundary between them and the action."[56] This boundary is part of the larger problem for Worthen, which he carefully unpacks as one of several outcomes of his foundational writing about *Sleep No More*. Worthen argues

---

[53] Freshwater, *Theatre & Audience*, p. 66.

[54] Mâchon, *Immersive Theatres*, p. 117; Worthen, *Shakespeare Performance Studies*, pp. 145, 143.

[55] Worthen, *Shakespeare Performance Studies*, pp. 142, 143.

[56] *Sleep No More*, production program, p. 24.

that audience members may "write our individualized plot lines in move-ment," but ultimately, we "are constructed within the spectacle as realist voyeurs, watchers, *readers*, not agents."[57] Worthen's contention is that *Sleep No More* is not really doing what it seems to be doing: Worthen only uses the term *immersive* in quotation marks, the implication being that *Sleep No More*'s dependence on realist concepts in its construction renders the audience merely roving watchers of conventional drama and the masks our own portable proscenium arches. For Worthen, the *Sleep No More* audience member may be physically close to the performers but is no more "immersed" than if seated in an auditorium.

This conclusion is echoed by scholar-artist Elizabeth (E. B.) Hunter. Hunter has written about what she calls "enactive spectatorship," in which the user or audience member has an active role to play (literally, as a character) in a performance or video game. During an engaging presenta-tion on her research, when asked about the difference between her game and *Sleep No More*, Hunter criticized the lack of interactivity in Punchdrunk's production with a punch line: "There's no *there* there."[58] Hunter's perspec-tive is not uncommon among those who think about immersivity: some expect a level of interactivity, the ability for the audience-participant – or user, in game design parlance – to affect the outcome of the performance. Hunter's "enactive" notion of spectatorship particularly validates the ways in which game play can amplify "the complex spectatorial position that arises out of collapsing actor and spectator."[59] By contrast, after Hunter "wandered through six floors of a witchy, film noir hotel," she concluded that "certain production choices construct a production-specific economy, where rewards that are valuable only within the world of that production replace *impact on the storyline* as the marker of an audience member's meaningful participation."[60] In other words, Hunter sees *Sleep No More* as an experience that offers rewards its audience-participants with experiences, but nothing as valuable to her as the opportunity to play a role in the narrative or influence its outcome.

---

[57] Worthen, *Shakespeare Performance Studies*, p. 144 (original emphasis).

[58] Hunter, presentation, Digital Shakespeares.

[59] Hunter, "Enactive Spectatorship," p. 7.   [60] Hunter, p. 6.

Hunter gave her aforementioned presentation via streaming video while sitting in a professional-looking office space that included a handsomely framed *Sleep No More* mask mounted on the wall behind her. Many studies that offer critiques of *Sleep No More* also acknowledge the "paradoxical" quality of the performance: that while the production is indebted to conventional, realist conceptions of dramatic writing (the construction of character, and audience regulation), it also "articulates an alternative, experiential, perhaps anti-interpretive paradigm of performance, as much of the choreography . . . fore-grounds performance as a *doing*, here and now, a practice we share with the performers," as Worthen concedes.[61] Presenting in front of her *Sleep No More* mask, Hunter tacitly acknowledged her place among the ranks of Worthen, Laura Levin, Paul Masters, Kathryn Prince, and others – scholars who offer forceful critiques of some of Punchdrunk's practices even while they also express a respect or even passion for *Sleep No More* and other Punchdrunk productions.[62] Prince's writing about *Sleep No More* is another example. She reports that *Sleep No More* "spectators' aimless wandering early in the evening quickly coalesces into hunting packs who chase the actors . . . jostling and shoving for the best view of an intimate moment of suffering or sex." Prince holds the production accountable for intentionally producing "Hobbesian" behavior among the entire audience.[63] Such exaggerations misrepresent the user experience of *Sleep No More* and the production that allegedly encourages such inhumane conduct. Further, such hyperbole detracts from Prince's more substantiated criticisms – that *Sleep No More* eschews "political purpose" to focus instead on marketing and "conspicuous consumption."[64] Yet, in the same article in which she claims that *Sleep No More* is designed to provoke antisocial conduct in the audience, Prince reports enjoying this "experimental, edgy, risky" production as a profound "sensory" experience; she even confesses that

---

[61] Worthen, *Shakespeare Performance Studies*, pp. 144–45 (original emphasis).

[62] Levin concludes that the *Sleep No More* audience performs "gendered labor." Levin, *Performing Ground*, p. 87. Hunter remarks that *Sleep No More* is "the gold standard of ableist scenic design." Hunter, ATHE Annual Conference (virtual, August 8, 2021).

[63] Prince, "Intimate and Epic," p. 254.

[64] Prince, "Intimate and Epic," pp. 255, 250.

its characters and scenes "haunted" her dreams (in a good way) for weeks.[65] These positive perspectives on *Sleep No More* by some of Punchdrunk's most forceful critics unexpectedly align with the claims of Mâchon and other Punchdrunk boosters. What do they all see in common?

Despite *Sleep No More*'s latent dependence on realist theatre and literary-Shakespearean convention, aspects of the production leap into a postdramatic register in which "ephemeral landscapes ... take the place of text"; these include the many dance sequences, detailed design and installation art, riveting task-based performances, and para-Shakespearean and Hitchcockian scenes in which (narrative) worlds collide to mesmerizing effect.[66] In these postdramatic performances, audience-participants watch actors "doing what they do," as Worthen puts it, in performances that go beyond the representational.[67] Indeed, *Sleep No More* "invites its audience to attend to actions done by actors in a performative environment," which means that its characters (Shakespearean and otherwise) are built "from the ecosystem up" rather than determined by textual sources.[68] As a result, the *doing* of the audience immersed in *Sleep No More* is reframed. Rick DesRochers places a premium on audience perception in the intimate spaces of immersive theatre: "Individuals' subjective responses *are* their participation in the performer-participant relationship."[69] Encountering spatialized characterization and task-based performance in this theatrical and citational ecosystem, audience-participants experience a "process-based spectatorship" that does more than simply resource the audience "as theatrical material for the show": it enables them as interactive co-creators of the performance. That felt experience of co-creative interaction contributes to a "state of *immersion*" through each audience member's negotiation of "space, sensation, and spectator."[70] As Carina E. I. Westling observes, the

---

[65] Prince, "Intimate and Epic," p. 250. [66] Masters, "Site and Seduction," p. 28.
[67] Worthen, *Shakespeare Performance Studies*, p. 139.
[68] Cook, *Building Character*, p. 117.
[69] DesRochers, "Immersive Performance," pp. 176–77 (original emphasis).
[70] Dinesh, *Memos from a Theatre Lab*, p. 122; Zaiontz, "Narcissistic Spectatorship," p. 406; Biggin, *Immersive Theatre and Audience Experience*, pp. 178, 33 (original emphasis).

theatre has always been a space that is both "structured *and* interactive," and Punchdrunk productions are no exception.[71] Similarly, Rose Biggin acknowledges – even validates – a wide spectrum for participation among examples of participatory performance: "Although interactivity may appear to be linked to immersive experience, many immersive productions are not particularly 'interactive' at all," at least not in the way that Hunter privileges. Biggin adds that some examples of immersive theatre "may include explicit participation in a *navigational* sense, but audience members are not invited to influence, change, or complete anything."[72] These degrees of participation are, for Biggin, part of the aesthetic of Punchdrunk's large-scale immersive shows.

The challenge for me is to find a way to resolve these seemingly incompatible views of a production that has emerged as the paradigm of immersive performance. One way to do so is offered by Jessica Pressman's process-based interpretation of the reading experience of Mark Z. Danielewski's novel *Only Revolutions* (2006). Pressman's discussion of how to read Danielewski's book provides a critical bridge in my thinking about audience experience in immersive narrativity. In her book *Digital Modernism*, Pressman concludes a study of digital literature by talking about a good old-fashioned book: Danielewski's novel *Only Revolutions* is a conventional book: ink on paper; but Pressman argues that *Only Revolutions* is nevertheless a product of new media thinking, in no small part because the book requires the reader to become "an interactive agent in fulfilling [its] potential."[73] The formatting of the novel is distinct: the main character in the narrative shifts from one side of the page to another; and the layout of words on the page is circular, so that the reader must turn the book in circles to read it, rendering the act of reading *Only Revolutions* into a "performance of its title." The format of the page draws attention to the act of reading and to the book itself, encouraging the reader to see this and other books "as a medium containing complex navigational structures and opportunities for interactivity."[74] Pressman's conclusion is that the reader

---

[71] Westling, *Immersion and Participation*, p. 9 (added emphasis).

[72] Biggin, *Immersive Theatre and Audience Experience*, p. 90 (added emphasis).

[73] Pressman, *Digital Modernism*, p. 174.

[74] Pressman, *Digital Modernism*, pp. 161, 173.

of *Only Revolutions* must play an active, participatory role in producing the book's meaning. The very same can be said for the audience-participant of *Sleep No More*.

True enough that an audience-participant cannot determine the outcome of *Sleep No More* any more than the reader of *Only Revolutions* can determine what's on the book's pages. Nevertheless, the audience-participant's active engagement is required to *fulfill the potential* of Punchdrunk's performance. Even if we cannot alter the production's outcome, the way that audience-participants engage the material produces each individual's experience of *Sleep No More*. Ultimately, the question of audience "emancipation" raised by Rancière and echoed by others is not about physical freedom, but about freedom of interpretation, regardless of what an audience-participant may physically do (or be permitted to do, or be discouraged from doing) during a performance. Altering the outcome of *Sleep No More* is not really the point: as Biggin puts it, "each spectator's progress creates an associative narrative," encountering a sequence of events that are, "the beginning, middle, and end *to them*."[75] To borrow from Pressman, the space of *Sleep No More* offers "complex navigational structures" that present its audience-participants with "opportunities for interactivity."[76] Navigating the spaces of immersive theatre and taking opportunities for interactivity are ways in which audience-participants fulfill the potential of performances like *Sleep No More*. Punchdrunk's performances encourage a particular kind of spectatorship: the practices of immersive theatre cultivate audience-participants who have the capacity to be active agents in their own narrative experiences.

Sleep No More and Its Prehistory

The practices of immersive theatre were not invented by Punchdrunk. The creators of *Sleep No More* and other immersive theatre makers – and there are many – have inherited a history of theatrical performances that try to

---

[75] Worthen, *Shakespeare Performance Studies*, pp. 85, 84; Biggin, *Immersive Theatre and Audience Experience*, p. 138 (original emphasis).

[76] Pressman, *Digital Modernism*, p. 173.

break down the conventions that separate audience space from performance space and that seek to place audiences and performers in a "shared space."[77] While experiments in theatre space have been continuously conducted from the 1950s to the present, the kinds of theatre that disrupt the boundary between audience and performance have a long historical legacy.

Immersive theatre engages with and is shaped by a long history of theatre that seeks to surround an audience with an engaging performance and to locate its audience in a dynamic performance environment. While several scholars offer selective surveys of influences on and precedents for Punchdrunk's immersive theatre, Carina E. I. Westling's study of Punchdrunk includes a substantial genealogy of immersive scenography. Her genealogy begins with the late nineteenth century and theatrical experiments "from Symbolism to Surrealism," and it draws an uninterrupted line to early twenty-first-century immersive productions. Westling tracks the "legacy" of European avant-garde "anti-realist modernism" across the twentieth century, shifting to "the postmodern perspective" in order to take in environmental, social, and participatory art experiments in Europe and North America.[78] Of particular interest to her are the post–World War II "Situationist art interventions" and Expanded Cinema exhibits that "blended interactivity and technology with performance."[79] Westling's project combines performance practice with analysis of scenographic design; what emerges is an account of the progressive shortening of the distance between audience and performer in theatrical space. This development in audience-performer relations (both physical and social) is key to the immersive aesthetic.

Westling uses the term *aesthetic* to good effect in her prehistory of Punchdrunk, deploying it to describe a set of ideas in development over a discontinuous span of time, rather than a smooth history of theatrical productions that are presented as inevitably coming to resemble what today is called immersive theatre. This focus on an aesthetic sensibility can reveal immersive theatre's connection to an even longer performance genealogy than

---

[77] Aronson, *History and Theory of Environmental Scenography*, pp. 7–8.

[78] Westling, *Immersion and Participation*, pp. 44, 47. For performance genealogy as historiographic methodology, see Roach, *Cities of the Dead*, pp. 25–31.

[79] Westling, *Immersion and Participation*, pp. 47–48, 57–58.

the 150 years that Westling traces, a genealogy that includes both historical contributors to the evolution of the immersive aesthetic, like medieval European Corpus Christi pageants and seventeenth-century European court performance; more recent precursors in this genealogy are more evident, like turn-of-the-millennium installations, performance art, and dance theatre.[80]

Mâchon takes a similar approach, identifying performance experiments that evince "a close affinity with the thinking and practice of current immersive theatre." Mâchon's focus is closer to the present; she begins from mid-twentieth-century Happenings (especially Allan Kaprow's theories and practice) and environmental performance in art and theatre. Notably, however, she also refers to "ancient and international rituals and theatre practices."[81] For Mâchon, including ritual as part of a genealogy of immersive performance is crucial because of what she views as immersive theatre's transformational potential: "the individual audience member influences the shape of the 'show'" by way of "active decision making," and in the course of the experience undergoes something "like a rite of passage." The spiritual connotations of Mâchon's claims of transformation or a "transfer of energy" strike me as uncritical, though they reflect the experience of Punchdrunk founder Felix Barrett himself.[82]

Barrett reports undergoing just such a transformational, rite-of-passage experience when he encountered installation art devised by renowned theatre director Robert Wilson. Artist and teacher Matthew Grant recounts this formative experience, in which Barrett attended Wilson's 1995 installation *H.G.*[83] *H.G.* was a twenty-room art piece in which the audience explored

---

[80] European court performance in particular should be seen as a formative site in the history of environmental, participatory performance. For the spatiality of English court performance, see Hopkins, "Reconsidering the Boredom of King James"; and Lin, *Shakespeare and the Materiality of Performance*. See also Claire Bishop, *Artificial Hells*; Bertie Ferdman, *Off Sites*; Hopkins, "A Concise Introduction to Immersive Theatre"; and Nick Kaye, *Site-Specific Art*.

[81] Mâchon, *Immersive Theatres*, pp. 31, 28.

[82] Mâchon, *Immersive Theatres*, pp. 28, 39.

[83] Wilson created *H.G.* in collaboration with Hans Peter Kuhn and Michael Howells. For descriptions of *H.G.*, see Mâchon, *The Punchdrunk Encyclopaedia*,

spaces independently, sometimes in groups, sometimes one at a time. Some spaces were detailed re-creations of realistic locations, while other rooms were more abstract environments of light and darkness, sound and imagery. As Grant recalls, after leaving *H.G.*, the teenage Barrett was stunned into silence for a long while: he "had clearly gone into that installation one person and came out as someone else."[84] While this tale has elements of hagiography, it would seem that in many ways, Barrett has been trying to re-create that formative experience (both the spatial encounter and its emotional impact) for his audiences. Thus, what might seem like an uncritical claim on the part of Mâchon may be more or less an explicit goal of Punchdrunk: to give audiences a transformational experience.

This potential for transformation would seem to be predicated on the liberatory function of the immersive experience. The *Sleep No More* website describes Punchdrunk's approach: "the company's infectious format rejects the passive obedience usually expected of audiences."[85] However, Masters, Worthen, and Zaiontz all separately claim that *Sleep No More* constrains rather than liberates its audience, arguing that the production surreptitiously applies spatial controls, offering its members only the appearance of freedom. Westling's design-focused study makes a counterargument: if *Sleep No More* is a kind of trap, then Punchdrunk gives its audience-participants the tools to find their way out. Westling sees in the spaces of *Sleep No More* much more than a "world of interiors": she sees a "design for agency," scenography that makes space for decision-making.[86] And both Masters and Worthen, while sometimes (highly) critical, identify numerous aspects of *Sleep No More* that are legitimately innovative and liberatory, freeing audience members "from the textuality of modern drama" and empowering them to "explore the anxious interplay of technology and

p. 133; Westling, *Immersion and Participation*, pp. 67–68; and Artangel (www.artangel.org.uk/).

[84] Quoted in Mâchon, *The Punchdrunk Encyclopaedia*, p. 127.

[85] "Hotel History," McKittrick Hotel website (https://mckittrickhotel.com/about/).

[86] Westling, *Immersion and Participation*, p. 70; "world of interiors" is from Brantley, "Shakespeare Slept Here."

site, time and space."[87] Thus, it would seem that what is key to the immersive aesthetic in general is key to the construction of *Sleep No More* as well: making space for agency and participation. In other words, while there are constraints and limits to being a Punchdrunk audience-ghost, there are affordances, too.

Ghosts and Ghosting in *Sleep No More*

The immersive aesthetic is about audience experience. While many discussions of *Sleep No More* describe what the performers do and what the performance environment looks like, the audience-participants should not be marginalized or neglected in the scholarship: what they do and how they navigate and perceive the dynamic environment is essential to the *Sleep No More* experience, even if most of the time audience-participants are silent witnesses, appearing to each other as ghostly masked faces in the background.

To return once more to Peter Holland's query about "ghosts in the audience": in pointing to the audience, Holland seems to have in mind the audience's own perceptual apparatus.[88] That is, the "ghosts," for him, are the quotations, themes, skeletons of dramatic structure, and other Shakespearean textual traces that audience members might bring with them to the theatre. These ghostly traces are the products of their reading and theatregoing experiences, and they might get deployed intuitively, informing interpretation as the audience members sit in their seats watching a play. But in the spatialized context of *Sleep No More*, I must ask again: *Where* are the ghosts? There are no seats for Punchdrunk's masked spectators – Mâchon's "*eerily* present witnesses," "spectres" roaming the dimly lit corridors – so literally locating the audience would be hard enough.[89] But there are multiple orders of ghost haunting this performance, and it's time to itemize them. While the text of Shakespeare's *Macbeth* may be foremost among the ghosts haunting the McKittrick Hotel, it's not alone among the different orders of ghost can be found in the spaces of *Sleep No More*.

[87] Masters, "Site and Seduction," pp. 28, 44.
[88] Holland, "Haunting Shakespeare," p. 212.
[89] Mâchon, "Watching, Attending, Sense-Making," p. 41.

The masked audience members are the first order: ghostly participants, they are present, active, decision-making agents of the performance who are mostly ignored by the characters, a performance practice that reinforces the perception that we are just ghosts wandering the McKittrick. The audience members' active engagement (choosing destinations, rummaging through filing cabinets, sprinting in the dark hallways) as perceiving, decision-making participants "fulfilling the potential," in Pressman's phrase, of the performance – which is to say, it would not be a performance without them.[90] Thus, being a *Sleep No More* audience member is complexly ghost-like: you can witness any part of the performance, and may at times be taken by the hand in a participatory moment, but the authority to determine the outcome of the performance will always slip through your fingers.

The second order of ghosts is a network of trace citations of Shakespearean dramatic literature. In the middle of an encounter that resembles a plot point in Macbeth, lines of text are heard whispered over a phone that has been pressed to an audience member's ear by a performer in a role that traces the contours of a Shakespearean character. Scenes like this abound in film versions and new stagings of Shakespeare, prompting Maurizio Calbi and many other theatre scholars to turn to the language of "hauntology": a critical effort to come to terms with the absent presence of a source or other influential material.[91] Calbi artfully compares Shakespearean hauntology to the ghost in *Hamlet*: "'here,' 'here,' and then . . . suddenly 'gone,' even though this disappearance often turns out *not* to be an absence." This is indeed how ghostly scraps of Shakespearean source material – "the spectral remainder of [Shakespeare's] language" – are distributed all over *Sleep No More*, rendering this immersive performance a literal "citational environment" in which audiences enter a space of text-based referentiality.[92] Thus, *Sleep No More* is a largely wordless *Macbeth* in which Shakespeare is disappeared but not absent, like a ghost.

---

[90] Pressman, *Digital Modernism*, p. 174.

[91] The term "hauntology" was coined by Derrida in *Specters of Marx* (1993 [trans. 1994]).

[92] Calbi, *Spectral Shakespeares*, pp. 6, 15, 144 (original emphasis). I love the phrase "citational environment," which Calbi borrows from Thomas Cartelli and Katherine Rowe. But Calbi, Cartelli, and Rowe all think of citational

But it is yet another order of ghosts in *Sleep No More* that is perhaps the most interesting to me: the media influences that make it a site in which "old media uncannily overlap with new media."[93] This third order of ghosting flips the script on what Calbi sees as "reciprocal haunting" in film appropriations of Shakespeare. Calbi writes that film versions of Shakespeare draw their "spectrality" from "the fact that they are media manifestations of Shakespeare" that put on film texts that were written for the stage.[94] While Calbi acknowledges that some films he considers result in an emphasis on an "empowerment of the body," in general he regards live performance to be part of the historical past. For Calbi, "the 'archaic' theatrical medium" is just another ghost that haunts film versions of Shakespeare.[95] Calbi's work opens up a discourse around Shakespearean hauntologies that frames the medium of theatre as a baseline point of reference, an archaic "thing" to be cited in films or other media, along with antiquated technologies like the typewriter or the gramophone. Thus, for Calbi, in common with many other Shakespeare scholars, the subject of their research is either a literary source or a media adaptation, while theatre is truly a ghost – a dead thing that haunts Shakespeare.

Sleep No More flips this script. The production is, of course, an embodied performance located in physical space, and this live immersive theatre performance is itself also haunted by other media, especially the structuring perspectives of cinema. The hauntology of *Sleep No More* then, is s system of meaning that deploys ghosts in the multiplicity of forms that I've described here: the audience-participants are framed as ghosts; ghostly textual references share space with the audience, smuggled in with the performers who also share that space; and the production is interwoven

---

environments as a purely textual: writing that includes citations to other (Shakespearean) writing. I appropriate this phrase to describe *Sleep No More* and other physical environments composed in part from Shakespearean citations.

[93] Calbi, *Spectral Shakespeares*, p. 18.

[94] Calbi, *Spectral Shakespeares*, p. 19 (added emphasis). Robert Shaughnessy observes more generally that even the most self-consciously cinematic examples of Shakespearean film still "value the ghosts of live performance." Shaughnessy, "Stage, Screen, and Nation," p. 59.

[95] Calbi, *Spectral Shakespeares*, p. 135.

with the subtle but no less influential ghosts of cinematic citation, including music, characters, locations, and references to specific films, not to mention the narrative practices of the movies, which are seen by the audience in the strategic approximation of camera action (establishing shots, close-ups, fade-outs, etc.). What I'm talking about when I talk about "ghosts" in *Sleep No More* is a network of paradoxical encounters experienced by the audience-participants of this immersive performance: actual encounters with things that aren't actually there – absent texts, media, and other source material – that nevertheless contribute to the meaning of a given moment and to the experience of the whole.

And, needless to say, a particularly spooky production of *Macbeth* in a vast, Hitchcock-themed haunted house is an apt context for a discussion of theatrical ghosting.

There is an expansive body of scholarly research that uses ideas of ghosts and the ghostly to explain the paradoxes of theatrical performance. This influential, decades-long scholarly discourse focuses on the idea of the ghost as an analogy for the theatre – an art form that is prone to appearances and disappearances.[96] Most studies reference Herbert Blau's *Take Up the Bodies: Theater at the Vanishing Point* (1982) as an early influence. Other studies include Alice Rayner's *Ghosts: Death's Double and the Phenomena of Theatre* (2006), Mary Luckhurst and Emilie Morin's collection *Theatre and Ghosts: Materiality, Performance, and Modernity* (2014), and Marvin Carlson's influential *The Haunted Stage: The Theatre as Memory Machine* (2001). In *Dark Matter* (2013), Andrew Sofer uses the phrase "spectral reading" to describe an interpretive strategy that not only looks for ghosts in the narrative of a play but also expands "the investigative spectrum" to consider influences on a play that are not immediately apparent to "the naked (critical) eye."[97] Sofer's hauntology is focused on the analysis of dramatic

---

[96] This last phrase surfaces a decades-long discourse on disappearance in the theatre, summed up by Thomas Postlewait, "Historiography and the Theatrical Event": "Because theater is an art form that disappears, historical scholarship is especially difficult." Postlewait, "Historiography and the Theatrical Event," p. 171.

[97] Sofer, *Dark Matter*, p. 9.

literature (it is "spectral *reading*" after all), but some theatrical performances get passing consideration in *Dark Matter*, including *Sleep No More*. For all these inquiries, thinking about theatre as inherently ghostly pushes performance to "remain in the space of the question, near the 'Who's there?' that famously opens *Hamlet*."[98] In this hauntological discourse of the stage, the "workings of performance become synonymous with the way in which the ghost operates," and "ideas of spectrality, ghosting, and haunting" are widely used "to interpret [the theatre's] production of meaning."[99]

Jessica Nakamura makes a valuable contribution to this discourse by pointing out not only that the discourse is overwhelmingly Western but also that most scholars in this discourse trace their model for theatrical ghostliness back to the ghost in *Hamlet*. Nakamura cites a wide body of work, confidently concluding that "*Hamlet*'s overwhelming influence on ideas of the spectral [is] known in theatre and performance studies."[100] She observes that even when voices in that discourse, like Marvin Carlson, acknowledge the "intensely haunted" tradition of Noh theatre, that tradition never becomes a source that informs general perspectives on ghosts in the theatre or theories of theatre itself as inherently ghostly. Nakamura's compelling corrective asserts the value of the Noh ghost both alongside other stage ghosts and indeed as a model for theatricality, "bringing global performance forms in conversation with existing theories."[101] In her analysis of sources from the Japanese tradition, the primary distinction that Nakamura offers is that "the appearance of the Noh ghost ... is not questioned [by other characters]" – as Hamlet does when he confronts the ghost of his father – "but rather engaged with as a real and forceful entity." Nakamura concludes: "this certainty distinguishes the Noh ghost from that of *Hamlet* and situates Noh's analytical potential in ghostly manifestation."[102] The theoretical implications of "certainty" in the face of an apparition are significant: "to read

---

[98] Riordan, "Ghosts," p. 167.

[99] Nakamura, "Against the Flows of Theory," p. 156.

[100] Nakamura, pp. 156, 166 n10. Riordan, "Ghosts," provides a fuller bibliography of hauntological theory, both theatrical and otherwise.

[101] Nakamura, "Against the Flows of Theory," p. 165.

[102] Nakamura, "Against the Flows of Theory," p. 158.

something onstage as (Noh) ghostly encourages us to think about ... the significances of the seen ghostly other," as well as "the significances of *seeing* the ghostly other."[103] As Nakamura frames it, the "(Noh) ghostly" is significant within a narrative context: the revelation of the ghost is usually coincident with the beginning of the resolution of the play. And that same "(Noh) ghostly" has a spectatorial significance as well: other characters – and the members of the theatre audience themselves – must recognize the (Noh) ghost as ghost.

The hauntology of *Sleep No More*, while not derived from Noh, can be explicated in part by Nakamura's analysis of the "(Noh) ghostly." Most of the time, characters in *Sleep No More* are seen by the audience members while the audience-as-ghost goes unseen by the characters. The ghosts here are dynamically present in the shared performance-audience spaces, taking the form of absent-but-perceivable textualities and media influences. The space of *Sleep No More* frames its audience members as ghosts twice over: figuratively, we are ghostlike because we walk, masked, among the spaces of *Sleep No More*, ignored by most of its characters; literally, we appear to one another as ghostlike extensions of the scenography, of a piece with the McKittrick's scenic design. Even more important, the work of *Sleep No More*'s audience-participants is in part to assemble an experience from among the different kinds of ghosts in the production. Audience members identify the supernatural characters in the narratives and spaces of *Sleep No More*, and are seen by them in turn; that act of seeing and recognizing is a ghostly experience itself. For the masked audience-participants of *Sleep No More*, we are ghosts watching ghosts.

Theatrical ghosting is a productive, even *performative*, kind of spectatorship: An audience member has to be able to recognize a meaningful (theatrical) relationship between what's there, materially, in a performance

---

[103] Nakamura, "Against the Flows of Theory," p. 160 (added emphasis). Nakamura uses the word *Noh* in parentheses, its presence ghosting the word *ghostly* that follows it. Nakamura's stated goal is for her study of the ghost in Noh to contribute to international (especially Western) theatre theory alongside Shakespeare-derived theories of theatre-as-ghostly.

and – more important – what's not. Mary Luckhurst and Emilie Morin see theatre as inherently spectral and spectators as "constantly engaged in interpreting acts of displacement and reconstruction."[104] The audience-participants' interpretation of Shakespearean source, contemporary performance, and classic cinema in the shared spaces of *Sleep No More* only enhances the sense of ghosting that Luckhurst and Morin identify as distinctly theatrical. *Sleep No More* is a Shakespearean citational environment populated by the ghostly traces of Shakespeare's language, the ghostly outlines of characters drawn from *Macbeth*, and the nonlinear ghosts of that play's narratives. At the same time, it is a cinematic citational environment populated with ghostly traces of film sources and structured by the signifying practices of cinema. For some theatregoers, the *Sleep No More* experience might amount to no more than walking around inside a building that curates a miscellaneous collection of dances, scenery, and references; the structuring function of director, choreographer, and designers might only incompletely give that miscellany any meaning. Such theatregoers may have a very satisfying evening at *Sleep No More*! However, the audience-participant who can assemble the elements of the performance into a meaningful experience and produce meaning is one who has cultivated a form of spectatorship adapted to spaces of theatrical ghosting – an *uncanny spectatorship*.

A capacity for uncanny spectatorship is essential to the navigation of a citational environment like *Sleep No More*, with its ghosts of Shakespearean textuality and other spectral traces. Indeed, uncanny spectatorship might be the necessary corollary to theatrical adaptation.

Unpacking the "Problem" of Adaptation

Not every play that references another source is engaged with theatrical ghosting. Sarah Bay-Cheng concludes a study of theatre and/as media with a critique of historiographies that "reconstruct an event as a 'ghostly' substitute for the performance that no longer exists."[105] In this discussion of *Sleep No More*, I am not using terms like *ghost* and *ghosting* nostalgically

---

[104] Luckhurst and Morin, "Introduction," p. 19.
[105] Bay-Cheng, "Theater Is Media," p. 40.

to describe long-lost theatre experiences. Rather, I deploy theatrical ghosting as a critical tool to describe performances that cite other (absent) performances, texts, or media. In these cases, pointing out absence is an adaptation strategy. Absence in these examples is not loss: what is absent is restored through some form of citation. The absent is still fundamentally *not there*, but it is also and at the same time *influencing what is there* – in this case, it does so in the context of a Shakespearean adaptation.

Beyond its explorations of the interior life of *Macbeth*'s characters or the thematic life of that play, *Sleep No More* offers something else as well. As Worthen argues, *Sleep No More* invokes *Macbeth* "as a means to creating a distinctive event, one that clearly depends on *Macbeth* but that exceeds, displaces, or avoids reduction to Shakespeare and his words." *Sleep No More*, Worthen concludes, both "is and is not *Macbeth*."[106] Thus, *Sleep No More* makes explicit what can be said of any performance of Shakespeare: it both is and is not reducible to its dramatic text. Further, while any immersive performance produces a unique, personal narrative that may be experienced as linear in terms of one's own embodied time,[107] in the case of *Sleep No More* that experience is the result of the audience's embodied navigation of a nonlinear adaptation – a spatialized performance of Shakespeare's linear play (among other source material). While it has features in common with the Wooster Group's *Hamlet* and other radical appropriations of Shakespeare, *Sleep No More* is a significant example of Shakespeare Performance in part because it so forcefully demonstrates that reception and interpretation are never more crucial than in the case of adaptation.[108]

Margaret Jane Kidnie's *Shakespeare and the Problem of Adaptation* establishes a firm foundation for dynamic perspectives on the relationship between text and performance in Shakespearean theatre. Kidnie takes a process-oriented approach to the subject, defining "a play" not as a stable, textual "fixed point" but as "a dynamic *process* that evolves over time in response to the needs and sensibilities of its users," and asserting that

---

[106] Worthen, *Shakespeare Performance Studies*, p. 86.

[107] Biggin, Immersive Theatre and Audience Experience, p. 138.

[108] See Hopkins, "Hamlet's Mirror Image," for a discussion of the Wooster Group's *Hamlet*.

the Shakespearean work "takes shape as a consequence of production."[109] From the outset of her 2009 book, Kidnie lays the groundwork for an argument that extends claims about Shakespeare's plays made decades earlier by Stephen Orgel. In his short but confrontational essay "What Is a Text?" (1981), Orgel argues that "a hard core of uncertainty" lies "at the heart of our texts" of Shakespeare's plays. At a time when theatre studies was still a hidebound field, Orgel, writing from a literary perch, argued that knowledge of early modern English theatre production must be incorporated into considerations of Shakespeare's plays. He concluded: "We know nothing about Shakespeare's original text"; instead, "the basic instability of the text" is an "essential" consideration for any future Shakespeare research.[110] Forty years later, these views are still not uniformly accepted, though they have been revisited in historical and theoretical studies by Orgel, Robert Weimann, and numerous other scholars.[111] Kidnie incorporates and advances these arguments in her study of the "problem" of adaptation. Kidnie's approach to adaptation proceeds from her definition of drama as "an art form that exists simultaneously in two media – text and performance." Kidnie acknowledges that adaptation "presents itself as an ongoing issue, or problem, *haunting* Shakespeare's plays."[112] It might be better to say, though, that the *problematic* of adaptation is an issue that haunts the *scholarship* of Shakespeare's plays, where the meaning-making relationship between text and performance has often been debated. Indeed, the "problem" of adaptation *is* the text versus performance debate.

Dennis Kennedy offers a kind of origin story for this debate. At the first performance of *Hamlet*, Shakespeare's play "was not a document but a set of vocalities and physical enactments inside a visual field." More than four hundred years later, Kennedy goes on, reception of Shakespeare Performance is a different matter: "a production of *Hamlet* ... arrives with history, heavy baggage strapped to the back of the performance, but chiefly loaded on reading, textual and biographical criticism, and the general

---

[109] Kidnie, *Shakespeare and the Problem of Adaptation*, pp. 2, 7 (original emphasis).
[110] Orgel, *The Authentic Shakespeare*, pp. 1, 5, 4.
[111] See especially Weimann, *Author's Pen and Actor's Voice*.
[112] Kidnie, *Shakespeare and the Problem of Adaptation*, pp. 6, 13 (added emphasis).

awareness of Shakespeare as an icon of high culture."[113] Audience reception of a given Shakespeare performance is complicated by an educational system focused on reading Shakespeare, to the point that for many the reception of Shakespeare in performance is perceived *as reading*. Of course, "going to Shakespeare" is not perceived that way by all theatregoers; Ric Knowles offers a more generous interpretation of what some Shakespeareans think about: "we go to watch a theatre company, at a particular historical and cultural moment, and using all of the representational technologies of theatrical production and performance (broadly understood), to engage with a rich representational history that includes all of the uses to which 'Shakespeare' and the particular script in question, have been put."[114] Still, though, Barbara Hodgdon sighs over her discontent with colleagues who cannot see the nuances of acting when they "go to Shakespeare," so intent are they on finding a reading experience in the theatre.[115]

The most noteworthy recent exchange in this ongoing critical debate is conducted in the context of a 2010 festschrift issue of *Shakespeare Yearbook* in honor of Robert Weimann, edited by David Schalkwyk. The key players in this exchange include Schalkwyk and Worthen, who both contribute chapters to this *Shakespeare Yearbook* volume, as does Weimann himself. Schalkwyk attempts to introduce the subject of the "struggle between text and performance" generously, though he proceeds to stake a "logical" claim for the literary side of the argument. Relying on speech act theory, he argues that the "language that makes up the text of *Hamlet*, however refashioned, shaped, appropriated, changed, pared down or expanded in production *remains* embodied in and through performance." In an aside, Schalkwyk claims that "reading is as much a performance as acting," a statement that encapsulates the thinking of the literary camp in the text and performance debate.[116] Indeed, the majority of Schalkwyk's contribution to this debate consists of critiques and rebuttals of Worthen's

---

[113] Kennedy, "The Spectator, the Text, and Ezekiel," p. 40.

[114] Knowles, "The Death of a Chief," p. 54.

[115] Hodgdon, quoted in Hopkins, "Hamlet's Mirror Image," pp. 20–21.

[116] Schalkwyk, "Text and Performance, Reiterated," pp. 49, 53, 71 (original emphasis).

previously published work on the subject, which "has explored how accepting the importance of fidelity to the assumed 'authority' of Shakespeare could constrain the work done by both performance practitioners . . . and performance critics."[117] In a rebuttal to Schalkwyk, Worthen's chapter lays out his foundational principle: "performance is not about conveying an encounter with a linguistic performative, but about the use of words in the creation of acts." He argues: "As *material*, the text is worked on and worked into the performance," and as a matter of historical evolution, "dramatic writing retains the potentialities we discover for its use."[118]

Weimann provides a way of moving past what might appear to be an (inter) disciplinary stalemate. In *Shakespeare and the Power of Performance*, Weimann and Douglas Bruster establish a kind of text-and-performance détente:

> In the absence of any traditionally fixed or given hierarchy between text and performance . . . it is helpful neither to overemphasize divisions and contestations of authority in the relations of these two media nor to postulate a given pattern of concurrence and complementarity between them. Instead, we propose to explore the extent to which . . . "actor's voice" is in "author's pen," but also . . . the ways and ends to which "author's pen" is in "actor's voice."[119]

The Weimann-Bruster perspective sidesteps the debate to emphasize specific examples, locating each theatrical performance in its historical and material circumstances. Worthen aptly summarizes Weimann's methodology: "how texts function in different conceptions of performance identifies what texts *are* and what *work they can do* in different conceptions of theatre."[120] Thus, Weimann and Bruster's negotiation of this problematic

---

[117] Bulman, "Introduction," p. 2.
[118] Worthen, "Shakespeare Performance Studies," pp. 82, 87, 86 (original emphasis).
[119] Weimann and Bruster, *Shakespeare and the Power of Performance*, p. 15.
[120] Worthen, "Shakespeare Performance Studies," p. 90 (original emphasis).

places an emphasis on the cultural and historical contingencies of performance and its interpretation.

Where Weimann artfully sidesteps the debate, Kidnie seems to want to bring it to a conclusion. Both scholars place a premium on reception: Weimann insists on the "perception of past significance through the inescapable lens of a present meaning," a phraseology that is a recurring refrain in his work; while Kidnie echoes this sensibility when she writes, "these works are entangled in the present ... *always* written again through production."[121] Kidnie's conclusion about Shakespeare Performance traces the contours of Weimann's past-and-present perspective while pointing toward her process-based approach to adaptation – one that validates theatrical performance. Kidnie's approach does not disrupt the textual authority of Shakespeare over a literary, reading experience of his texts; rather, her argument simply admits another order of meaning-making, with an alternative order of authority over that meaning. Her succinct (if provisional) resolution to the text versus performance debate derives from her deceptively simple definition of "drama" as something rooted in their duality. This understanding grants the Shakespearean text a double life, which Kidnie finds in the "unpredictable and never finally completed interplay between production and *reception*."[122] Can solutions to the text/performance problematic be found in the relationship between an adaptation and its audience?

Despite numerous forays into this text/performance struggle, no amount of logical argumentation seems to have won Kidnie or Worthen (let alone Weimann or Orgel) much ground against Schalkwyk and other literary Shakespeareans. I'm certainly aligned with the latter-day champions of Orgel's early disruptive claims. This Element – indeed, all my research and teaching – views Shakespeare as "an ongoing process of textual-theatrical evolution." The argument has evolved from Orgel's assertion of the fundamental instability of the Shakespearean text to "a critical awareness of the work as process," an awareness that shifts the emphasis

---

[121] Weimann, "Performance in Shakespeare's Theatre," p. 4; Kidnie, *Shakespeare and the Problem of Adaptation*, p. 102 (original emphasis).

[122] Kidnie, *Shakespeare and the Problem of Adaptation*, p. 102 (original emphasis).

of Shakespeare Performance research "from what one knows now to what one might be able to recognize in the future as Shakespeare's works."[123] The text and performance problematic will likely endure because the positions taken in the debate often seem to reflect disciplinary understandings (literature studies and performance/theatre studies) as much as claims in an isolated argument. However, this debate is worth considering because the study of Shakespeare is exemplary of the study of textuality in the theatre. Shakespeare "provides a paradigm of performance, at least a paradigm of those forms of performance using writing as one instrument of performing."[124] Placing a premium on reception surfaces multiple solutions to the text/performance problematic, at least for those willing to abide multiple equally valid sources of Shakespearean meaning.

Punchdrunk avoids referring to *Sleep No More* as an adaptation, as Elizabeth Hunter observes: "from the show's website, to its lush, seventy-page handbook, to transcriptions of Shakespeare's dialogue, *Sleep No More* studiously avoids the term 'adaptation' and takes great pains to foreground its canonical source."[125] This observation surprises me – it runs counter to my perception of *Sleep No More* as an iconoclastic adaptation. Worthen argues that a traditional relationship with dramatic text lurks just beneath *Sleep No More*'s dance theatre iconoclasm, and his argument aligns with Kennedy's general observation about Shakespearean appropriations: "when a production tries to sidestep the baggage of history by offering a radically new or oppositional interpretation, the result is likely to call further attention to the *ghostly* traces of the play's past, ironically foregrounding it as a literary document in the midst of its deconstruction."[126] Hunter goes so far as to argue that a concern with an "authentic" literary source material is not *beneath* the production's surface but *on* its surface: "Shakespearean authenticity is central to *Sleep No More*'s aesthetic. Of the many mysteries the show works hard to cultivate, the production's identification with *Macbeth* is not

---

[123] Orgel, *The Authentic Shakespeare*, p. 5; Kidnie, *Shakespeare and the Problem of Adaptation*, p. 102.

[124] Worthen, *Shakespeare Performance Studies*, p. 88.

[125] Hunter, "Enactive Spectatorship," p. 15n19.

[126] Kennedy, "The Spectator, the Text, and Ezekiel," p. 41 (added emphasis).

an element it wishes to obscure."[127] Indeed, it may seem that Punchdrunk is contradicting itself, trying to have it both ways in its marketing: presenting *Sleep No More* as something new and innovative while also emphasizing that it is Shakespeare. However, Punchdrunk's investment in *Sleep No More* as "authentic Shakespeare" is not contradictory to its identity as immersive dance theatre adaptation.[128] The historical ghosts that Kennedy sees in performance result from the frictions of adaptation. *Sleep No More*'s status as adaptation is essential to understanding it as Shakespearean. It's where the ghosts come from.

For all these reasons, I use the term "adaptation" to refer to *Sleep No More*. This is not the only term that might be used, though. Julie Sanders helpfully disambiguates *adaptation* and *appropriation*, and from her perspective, *Sleep No More* might well be the latter. But I'm sticking with the former for two reasons. First, in contemporary theatre, adaptation is more often than not what a production of a classic play looks like – even granted that exactly what might be called a "production of" a source text may vary widely, as John Rouse astutely points out.[129] Theatre productions that fall under the rubric of what Hans-Thies Lehmann terms the *postdramatic* depend on a loose and flexible relationship with a source text, and *Sleep No More* is a significant example of the postdramatic.[130] Referring to this diverse range of productions of canonical texts as "appropriations" rather than simply "productions of" those texts strikes me as a bit reductive. Adaptations are not the exception in theatre, they are the rule. Indeed, Sanders effectively avoids the controversy around Shakespeare adaptation by describing adaptation as characteristic of Shakespeare's plays themselves. Subsequently, her discussion of contemporary adaptations of Shakespeare's plays is framed as perfectly logical. There is a lively discourse around Shakespeare adaptation that includes decades of stage-and-screen

---

[127] Hunter, "Enactive Spectatorship," p. 15n19.
[128] See Orgel's indispensable discussion of the myth of an "authentic Shakespeare," *The Authentic Shakespeare*.
[129] Rouse, "Textuality and Authority," pp. 146–58.
[130] Lehmann, *Postdramatic Theatre*; and Worthen, *Shakespeare Performance Studies*, pp. 3–8.

study and, more recently, scholarship of new media Shakespeares. Quite simply, I want to locate my discussion of *Sleep No More* in relation to that adaptation discourse. Adaptation – as a critical concept and a creative practice – decouples a theatrical performance from its Shakespearean source; for some creators and audience members, this is a liberating act, while for others this decoupling surfaces anxious concerns about so-called "authenticity."

"Authenticity" is a canard, as Orgel has definitively concluded; it is a term that I feel compelled to use in scare quotes. Yet, many scholars still view ephemeral stage performances as travesties of an "authentic" written text, as Barbara Hodgdon has observed ruefully.[131] Bulman, like Kidnie, is concerned with "the *problem* of what constitutes 'Shakespeare' in the theatre today." He asserts that adaptations "focus the *problem* most clearly." However, the rhetoric of Bulman's discussion of adaptation escalates, and it becomes clear that, for Bulman, adaptations of Shakespeare are indeed a problem, especially in the case of "experimental performance practices."[132] As an example, Bulman singles out *Sleep No More*, which he criticizes as "*unmoored* from its Shakespearean source."[133] By contrast, Sanders's discussion of adaptation dives into the subject with a real enthusiasm for the "reinterpretative act." Sanders loosely defines her subject as "reinterpretations of established texts," which may include "relocations of an 'original' or sourcetext's [sic] cultural and / or temporal setting."[134] She concludes that "it is the very endurance and survival of the sourcetext that enables the ongoing process of juxtaposed readings that are crucial to the cultural operations of adaptation, and the ongoing experiences of *pleasure* for the reader or spectator in tracing the intertextual relationships." Among the strengths of Sanders's wide-ranging study of adaptation and appropriation is the unabashed joy she finds in her examples. The word *pleasure* occurs frequently in her study, as she herself acknowledges: "I make no apologies for introducing pleasure into the equation."[135] While "pleasure"

---

[131] Hodgdon, "Scholar Spotlight." [132] Bulman, "Introduction," p. 3.
[133] Bulman, "Introduction," p. 3.
[134] Sanders, *Adaptation and Appropriation*, pp. 2, 19.
[135] Sanders, *Adaptation and Appropriation*, pp. 25, 17.

may seem to be an uncritical term, I consider it to be especially relevant in a study of a popular adaptation like *Sleep No More*. While many studies of Shakespeare adaptation compare an adaptation to the "original" to identify what was done *to* Shakespeare, Kidnie and Sanders (along with Barrett, Bloom, Cook, Worthen, and other voices in the bibliography of this Element) are more concerned with what was done *with* Shakespeare: What new concepts or conditions are being explored or produced in the context of an adaptation in performance?

Opposing what Kidnie terms a "problem" with what Sanders sees as a pleasure opens up avenues for research inquiry. Sanders's approach shifts the interpretive authority for adaptation to reception, to the reader or spectator, which in theatrical performance means that the authority for meaning-making resides in the audience. An audience member's immediate pleasure and independent interpretive faculties balance what they may retain of the complex admixture of history, criticism, and cultural iconicity aptly diagnosed by Kennedy. With this shift, a Shakespeare adaptation has the potential to conduct interrogative work in performance, to intervene in contemporary culture, and to step beyond the presumption that performances of Shakespeare should do no more than offer insights into Shakespeare. Indeed, despite some differences in terminology, Kidnie's and Sanders's perspectives closely align. Both clearly take *pleasure* in the *problem* of Shakespeare adaptation.

Crucial for my discussion of *Sleep No More*, Sanders explores the "textual ghosting" that is an inherent aspect of adaptations: for an audience experiencing a Shakespearean "work," comparison with other instances of that work is inevitable, "fundamental, even vital." The many "textual ghosts and hauntings" that Sanders sees in adaptations are entirely desirable, the products of "reinterpretations of established texts."[136] This textual ghosting is most directly felt in the moments of absence: it is the recognition that expected text from a familiar source is not "there" for the audience to find in a given performance, even though the performance traces the contours of that text. For those who can see what's not there, meaningful acts of adaptation emerge from deletions, elisions, and other forms of

---

[136] Sanders, *Adaptation and Appropriation*, pp. 19, 32.

absence. Admittedly, absence will only be recognized as such by people who know what might have been "there." Seeing such ghosts is an interpretive act: apprehending signification in a carefully structured negative (textual) space.

For *Sleep No More* audience members who can't play along with its practices of textual ghosting – those who can't see what they're missing – then the (textual) ghosts just won't be visible. Those audience members may not functionally be attending an adaptation of *Macbeth*. Instead, they will merely be audience-participants at an immersive dance theatre show in a spooky haunted house–like environment – and that's ok, too. But for those who can see what's not there, this practice of seeing ghosts ("the ongoing experiences of ... tracing the intertextual relationships" in an adaptation) is a source of pleasure, and indeed it's the source of what is Shakespearean in *Sleep No More*.[137] Seeing ghosts in the theatre is another act of participation on the part of the audience-participant: it's essential to the uncanny spectatorship of Shakespeare adaptation. Beyond navigating its many spaces, the primary activity of the *Sleep No More* audience-participant, then, is (re)interpretation: identifying the ghostly traces of dramatic, theatrical, and cinematic sources that haunt the McKittrick.

Gamification and *Sleep No More*

The thrill that I got from experiencing the Secret Sixth Floor of *Sleep No More* was in no small part the thrill of figuring out how to get a performer to take me to the Secret Sixth Floor. Most *Sleep No More* attendees will have no idea that there is a Secret Sixth Floor. (Because "secret.") Unlike most of the other locations in the sprawling performance complex, audience members must be chosen by a performer to ascend to the Sixth Floor, and the selection process may seem arbitrary. Punchdrunk's one-on-ones are always initiated by a performer, and even though experienced *Sleep No More* audience members can try to finesse certain outcomes, nothing is guaranteed. Recall my earlier anecdote about *not* getting chosen to go to the Secret Sixth Floor. That was the first time I tried to "play" *Sleep No More* in

---

[137] Sanders, *Adaptation and Appropriation*, p. 25.

order to produce a particular result.[138] Though frustrated on that occasion,
I was determined to try again.

I returned to New York City a year later. I was in the first group to exit
the Manderley Bar and enter the *Sleep No More* space proper, because I'd
finagled that ace from "Mr. Hopkins" at reception. About a dozen of us
crowded in front of the elevator, listening to instructions from one of the
costumed hosts. Upstairs, I exited the elevator and quickly refamiliarized
myself with what was where in the sprawling performance complex. My
primary goal for this visit to *Sleep No More* was to get to the Sixth Floor.
From my previous visit, I was confident that I needed to be in the fifth-floor
hallway outside the hospital, and that I needed to be there early in the
performance. I went directly to the hospital and lingered in the doorway,
watchful. At about quarter after the hour, which I thought was ahead of
schedule, I started to feel that standing around waiting was a waste of
precious *Sleep No More* research time, so I walked downstairs one flight to
further reorient myself to the multistory performance space. Mistake!
I nearly missed my chance.

Coming back up to the fifth floor about five minutes later, I immediately
saw a performer coming toward me down the corridor outside the hospital:
she was wearing a black overcoat and carrying an old-fashioned suitcase. I'd
seen this enigmatic character at past visits to *Sleep No More*; some fans call
her "the Sixth Floor Nurse." She spotted me as soon as I walked back in
from the stairwell, and she froze. I froze, too – this was the character I'd
been waiting for. I wanted to run to her and say, "Pick me! Let's go!" There
were no audience members around, it seemed, but I felt that I had to play
a role of sorts – I didn't want to scare her off. So I actually took a half step
back, as if I were a reluctant participant, unsure what to expect. The Sixth
Floor Nurse took a few quick steps toward me, and I took a couple steps
toward her, too, though more tentative. She promptly closed the distance
and reached out her hand expectantly. I hesitated just a moment before

---

[138] Information can be found online about the places in The McKittrick where
audience-participants can try to initiate one-on-ones. In my case, the
gamification began in the bar: I elicited advice from two costumed hosts in The
Manderley by playing the part of a "hotel guest."

raising my hand. Was I acting? I didn't think of it as "acting" at the time: I was participating in a dynamic situation, and I wanted to achieve a particular outcome. A moment later, she abruptly grabbed my hand, stepped close, and grabbed my other hand, too. Holding both my hands, she looked deeply into my eyes – I was, of course, still wearing a white mask over my face – and then turned. I fought the urge to respond with a very strong grip for fear of being left behind, but there was no need: she held on to me tightly and led me briskly into the stairwell.

We passed another audience member who I think was trying to join us. With my peripheral vision so limited by the mask, I focused on the steep stairs with the performer running in front of me, pulling me along. She never slowed as we went up to a landing, past a black-masked usher, and up one last flight to the sixth floor and a steel door. I looked back and could see the usher shaking her head, blocking the other audience member from following us. Sorry, friend – I know the feeling. At the top of the stairs, just outside the door, the light was dim. As I turned back from looking over my shoulder, I nearly walked into the door that the Sixth Floor Nurse had just opened. She turned to me and quietly warned, "Be careful." (Was it the character whispering to me, or the actor?) Then, taking my hand again, she led me through the door.

As the performer led me to the Secret Sixth Floor, the moment felt unreal, because it was more or less exactly how I'd imagined it would look and feel. For me, getting taken to the Secret Sixth Floor was the best part of the Secret Sixth Floor experience. This is no criticism of the conception of that scene, nor of the fine performances, installation art, and design that I saw there; rather, it's an acknowledgment of the thrill that I got from such active participation in my own immersive experience. I was clearly co-performing in a theatre event that already relies heavily on audience engagement. Indeed, the only reason I have seen the Sixth Floor (twice) is because I schemed to get myself there over multiple visits to *Sleep No More*. The fact that it worked out (in two out of four attempts) is a source of personal satisfaction. This feeling itself is a research finding: one of the things I have most enjoyed in multiple visits to *Sleep No More* is something that I did in active participation with the performance: essentially *playing* the performance like a game.

Getting taken to the Secret Sixth Floor of *Sleep No More* is an example of what Gina Bloom refers to as the "gamification" of Shakespeare Performance: something that you might try to finesse or make happen in the context of an immersive theatre experience. The fact that my intentions could determine the outcome of part of my experience was the height of immersive interactivity, and this outcome exemplifies Bloom's arguments about gamification and performance. Indeed, Bloom redefines theatre as "one of the earliest media technologies for interactive play."[139] Bloom's discussion focuses on the early modern English commercial theatre in which Shakespeare's plays were first produced. By looking at both the history of games like chess and the representation of those games in Shakespeare's plays, Bloom is able to frame early modern drama as "playable media," whether in the context of early modern theatre or in a conventional contemporary staging. Bloom conceives of theatre as "an information game played between its producers and audiences," one that makes "room for the audience's participatory energies."[140] Her argument is that all theatre can be "played" in this way – and maybe already is. Bloom's study of the gamification in and of early modern drama offers valuable perspectives when turned to a consideration of immersive theatre and its audience. *Sleep No More* can be seen as "playable Shakespeare" in which meaning is produced not merely through the actors' performances, which is true of all theatre, but through the actions of the audience-participants as well. As I've already explained, an audience member's experience of an immersive production like *Sleep No More* simply doesn't happen without the active participation of that audience member. Bloom's perspective shows *Sleep No More* as game space whose meanings are not just knowable to but produced by the "play" of those within the McKittrick.

The effect of putting game play at the center of a theory of theatre is that the audience is rendered as "a kind of living archive" of theatre experience. For Bloom, "plays and/as games accentuate the body as a site of knowledge

---

[139] Bloom, *Gaming the Stage*, p. 1. Bloom's book shares perspectives with Alan Galey's *The Shakespearean Archive*: both offer a media archeology perspective on aspects of Shakespeare Performance.

[140] Bloom, *Gaming the Stage*, pp. 175, 18, 19.

production and acquisition."[141] Not just some abstract body – *your* body. That an actor's body is a site of meaning in performance is a self-evident feature of theatre; what is innovative in Bloom's argument is her claim that audience members' bodies, too, are productive sites of theatre knowledge. If you as a theatregoer can be a living archive of embodied theatre meaning, what exactly gets stored in your body? If certain kinds of Shakespeare Performance make forms of knowledge production explicit, then the knowledge that they produce is the consequence of audience participation in those performances. The goal is not to "win" theatre; rather, the goal is to be able to do things with and within a theatre experience – whether for an early modern audience or a contemporary one.[142] Thus, the gamification of theatre is not of peripheral concern to performance research: it is the key to how Shakespeare's plays function as "strange tools," in Noë's phrase, for the production of new knowledge, knowledge centered in audience experience.[143]

One way in which audience members serve as an archive in relation to *Sleep No More* and other appropriations of Shakespeare's texts is that we bring with us the words that aren't spoken in the performance. True, most audience members don't have *Macbeth* memorized, and I'm not sure it would actually help if they did. However, a knowledge of Shakespeare's play brings with it certain affordances for an audience member, including the potential to interpret characters encountered, locations entered, and the things that happen in them. Punchdrunk, in common with other immersive companies, often draws on classic texts as source material.[144] The presumption seems to be that a familiar story, including some knowledge of the characters in it, will

---

[141] Bloom, *Gaming the Stage*, p. 174. See also Bloom, Bosman, and West, "Ophelia's Intertheatricality."

[142] This discussion of audience as site for the production, storage, and recall of knowledge invokes Diana Taylor's *The Archive and the Repertoire*. Among numerous evaluations of Taylor's work, see Worthen, "Antigone's Bones"; Schneider, *Performing Remains*, pp. 87–110; and Hopkins, "Reconsidering the Boredom of King James."

[143] See Noë, *Strange Tools*.

[144] See Mâchon, *The Punchdrunk Encyclopaedia*, pp. 272–75.

provide an audience member with a frame of reference in an unfamiliar environment. Barrett makes this very point: a Punchdrunk production "might be experientially challenging in its non-linear form so the source becomes a navigational tool."[145] Thus, while the immersive participant is trying to navigate the space and learn its rules, prior knowledge of the classic source may serve as a map or guide of sorts. Sanders questions "whether or not knowledge of a source text is required or merely enriching" when exploring an unfamiliar adaptation; she acknowledges that it's a complicated question. It's certainly a question my students often ask.[146] Bloom's work proposes something other than a yes/no answer to that question: the notion that by recognizing their role in the performance, "theatregoers could become more competent at theatre," honing their "theatregoing skills."[147] This means that someone who has not read *Macbeth* may still enjoy *Sleep No More* and form deep meanings there. Indeed, I think *Sleep No More*'s popularity relies on its appeal to people who are not "fluent" in Shakespeare. But someone who is familiar with *Macbeth* will have a deeper appreciation of scenes, characters, and action, even the environments: they will have more information than others in the "information game" that is playable Shakespeare, and so they will have more *pleasure*, as Sanders writes, in "tracing the intertextual relationships."[148] Here we see the gamification of Shakespeare Performance: audience members who have *Macbeth* at their fingertips to one degree or another will have different capacities to interpret their experiences of *Sleep No More*, and the result will be a different – and perhaps a deeper – engagement with this performance and its meanings. In short, the more you know about its Shakespearean source, the more fun you'll have playing (at) this immersive experience.

Bloom concludes her redefinition of Shakespearean drama as game by arguing that theatrical performance presents "the play as an opportunity for play."[149] What would "playing a play" look like? How might one "play"

---

145 Quoted in Mâchon, *The Punchdrunk Encyclopaedia*, p. 272.

146 Sanders, *Adaptation and Appropriation*, p. 23.

147 Bloom, *Gaming the Stage*, pp. 172, 175.

148 Bloom, *Gaming the Stage*, p. 18; Sanders, *Adaptation and Appropriation*, p. 25.

149 Bloom, *Gaming the Stage*, p. 19.

Sleep No More? In response, I'll describe the time I accidentally discovered how to get escorted out of *Sleep No More* by Lady Macbeth herself.

The finale of *Sleep No More* has been described already: at the end of the performance, the audience gathers around to observe the third iteration of the banquet scene and the fatal end of Macbeth's last "loop." In the first two iterations of the banquet, Lady Macbeth stands in slow motion, then, at the end of the sequence, she is among the first to dash off. But in the third and final iteration of the banquet, Lady Macbeth exits stage left (the banquet is the only point in *Sleep No More* when there's actually a stage to refer to), and while attention is directed up and stage right to Macbeth's last moments, she surreptitiously joins the audience, standing among the front row and watching her husband's fate. In the near darkness that follows Macbeth's death, Lady Macbeth turns to the audience-participant on her left, slowly raises her hand while making significant eye contact, and then formally leads that audience member from the room and back to the Manderley Bar while the rest of the audience mills along behind.[150]

The first time I had this experience, I turned from Macbeth's demise, seeing motion on my right in the dim light, only to discover Lady Macbeth looking right at me, and reaching out. On this occasion, the performer was Tori Sparks, an early, influential interpreter of *Sleep No More*'s Lady Macbeth. Sparks took my hand and led me back to the Manderley Bar at a stately pace; there, she turned me so that my back was against the wall of a quiet corner; she gently lifted off my mask; she kissed me lightly, high on the left cheek, and whispered in my ear: "Welcome back." Years later, I had a similar experience at *Sleep No More* in Shanghai, where the fictional hotel venue is called the McKinnon. The integrated cast of the Shanghai

---

[150] I was escorted out by Lady Macbeth twice. When *Sleep No More* reopened after the COVID shutdown, the typical one-on-ones were put on hold, and these post-show "escort" opportunities were multiplied. On one occasion, I was led out by Hecate, very much in character: she took my hand, starting at a slow walk; soon she was dragging me through the space at a sprint, cackling wildly; once, she looked back to see whether I was having trouble keeping up. (Who looked back? The character or the actor?) Then, with a wicked grin, she squeezed my hand and raced ahead again.

production included actors whom my Chinese friends described as either "Asian" or "European," in reference to the apparent heritage of the performers. On the occasion that I attended, my friends told me afterward that they were surprised to see a "European" Lady Macbeth. She was the best I've seen in the role since Sparks – more actor than dancer, which brought a richness to the emotional life of the character's wordless performance, even if her dancing was less virtuosic than performances I've seen at the McKittrick. At the McKinnon, I followed Lady Macbeth for her last loop, which ended as it always does, at the banquet. As I watched the conclusion of the performance, it occurred to me that there might be one more opportunity for a kind of one-on-one. As Macbeth prepared for his death scene and lights dimmed to focus attention on him, I was standing on the right side of the ballroom opposite Lady Macbeth's stage left position. Black-masked ushers directed the audience to back away from the low stage on which the banquet table is set, but I held my position: as if I were just being polite, I gestured for others to go past me, though my intentions were not altruistic. After I "graciously" allowed other audience members past me, I was left standing at the front of the audience directly opposite Lady Macbeth. As the last moments of the performance occurred, I watched her step off the stage. She immediately walked over and stood next to me on my right, watching Macbeth along with everyone else. Why? Had I positioned myself just right? Maybe. Did she remember me as the attentive-but-respectful audience-participant in her last loop? Maybe. We'd had an interaction during that loop: in one of the character's manic moments – the only time when non-supernatural characters can "see" the otherwise ghostly audience members – Lady Macbeth grabbed my lapel and turned me in a brief dance as other audience members watched.[151] Did she remember me? Maybe. Or maybe this is just where she always stands, and I was lucky to be in the right place. Either way, my effort to "play" *Sleep No More* made possible what followed. As Macbeth met his end, I was watching Lady Macbeth out of the corner of my eye. I played the moment

---

[151] Characters in *Sleep No More* only "see" audience-participants "if [they] are magical, in a state of madness, or ghosts." Punchdrunk collaborator Katy Balfour, quoted in Mâchon, *The Punchdrunk Encyclopaedia*, p. 205.

much the way I did when trying to get taken to the Secret Sixth Floor: I didn't want to appear too eager, so I was careful not to get caught looking at her before she turned to look at me. Upon Macbeth's death, as all eyes in the crowd were directed upward, Lady Macbeth turned in slow motion to look at me; she raised her hand to me, just as slowly. Minutes later, in a dim corner of the bar, I can remember hearing background chatter in Mandarin as Lady Macbeth whispered in American-accented English, "Welcome back."

The rare opportunity to interact with Lady Macbeth at the finale of *Sleep No More* finds a kind of counterexample in the character of Hecate. Hecate has her own space in *Sleep No More*, and while this character's actions loop the way other characters' do, Hecate spends a good deal of her time in a single location, the so-called Dead Bar (Figure 7). The Dead Bar is

Figure 7 Hecate in the "Dead Bar." Photo: Umi Akiyoshi for The McKittrick Hotel.

a sinister doppelganger of the Manderley Bar. Visitors to the Dead Bar can watch Hecate perform a sequence of actions, most of which have nothing directly to do with Shakespeare's tragedy but evoke a sense of this Shakespearean character, goddess of witchcraft. Attired in a lipstick-red ball gown, Hecate combines silent film–era glamour with a malevolent sense of humor. The paisleysweets authors have advanced a theory that Hecate is in fact the defining character of the McKittrick Hotel, the one who causes the worlds of Shakespeare and Hitchcock to collide and loop in a repetitive nightmare. The authors' argument is well supported, the product of many hours of fieldwork at *Sleep No More*. They document the characters who pass through Hecate's space, arguing that it is she who makes these (narrative) worlds collide.[152] But regardless of how one sees her role in the grand, nonlinear scheme of things, Hecate's "dead" version of the Manderley offers another spatial and narrative nexus in *Sleep No More*. Indeed, several characters' loops pass through Hecate's Dead Bar, most notably the witches (who are servants of Hecate) and, of course, Macbeth himself (Figure 8).

Audience-participants linger in the Dead Bar to take advantage of uninterrupted time with a single character: Hecate's performance encompasses several task-based activities including a lip-synched torch song and a gruesome meal. Hecate's Dead Bar is one of the most active sites for audience-character interaction. Because Hecate spends so much time here, there are continual opportunities for participation at various scales, from simply making eye contact as she walks past to being selected for a one-on-one in her lair. Hecate is among the most famous purveyors of one-on-ones in *Sleep No More*, and audience-participants can be seen trying to access one of these performances: a corrugated metal door leads to Hecate's private chamber, and audience members are occasionally led into this "lair." This is one of the locations in *Sleep No More* where audience members can linger with extended access to a single character; and, in this case, it's a character who can in turn see the audience members. Unlike the non-supernatural

---

[152] Paisleysweets, "Once Upon a Time." In this same blog post, the authors astutely point out that the Porter in the hotel lobby has a Norman Bates-like connection with Hecate, though the characters never directly interact.

Figure 8 "Bald Witch" dancing with Macbeth. Photo: Umi Akiyoshi for The McKittrick Hotel.

characters, who can only see audience members when in extreme psychological states (Lady Macbeth toward the end of her loop, for example), the supernatural characters (Hecate and the witches) can see and interact with audience members all the time. Hecate seems to take pleasure in teasing or otherwise performing audience members, and significant eye contact is a notable part of the character's repertoire. These factors combine to make Hecate's Dead Bar the most "playable" location in the participatory ecosystem of *Sleep No More*. So playable, in fact, that Hecate's one-on-one often occurs in two parts.

I've experienced the one-on-ones with Hecate multiple times, both at The McKittrick in NYC and at The McKinnon in Shanghai. In its ideal form, one-on-one interaction with Hecate happens in two parts. The first one-one-one is brief Hecate leads you into her lair – a darkly cozy sitting room —then she leans in close and whispers instructions to deliver a note to the Porter in the lobby. She hands over a note (signed with a bright red lipstick kiss), then guides the audience-participant back out the door. For those willing to play this game-within-the-play, Hecate's assignment introduces a task-oriented form of audience-ing to the otherwise unstructured experience of *Sleep No More*. If you deliver Hecate's message to the Porter, he sends word back to her in the form of a note folded into the shape of a boat. Returning with the paper boat rewards the participant with a more substantial private audience in Hecate's lair. Like the one-on-one with the Matron, Hecate's second, much longer, one-on-one features a tea party – one that quickly turns from charming to menacing. The first time I experienced this one-on-one, a story was told about a ship and a storm, a lot of tea got spilled on me, the paper boat message was dropped in my teacup, unread; and then things got surprisingly bloody – all very much on brand for Hecate. Subsequently, I was dragged into a completely dark secondary space where Hecate cackled and shouted a threatening monologue; in the dark, my hands were grabbed and forced to explore a wall overgrown with unseen plant matter while it rained on me. Finally, I was pushed out a another door. (In Shanghai, I was roughly shoved into a hallway bare-faced for long seconds before my mask was unceremoniously tossed on the floor in front of me. Other audience members assumed I was a performer and followed me for a while, even after I had my mask back on.) In Hecate's second one-on-one, the audience member experiences what it's like to be on the receiving end of this character's manipulative, theatrical cruelty. But the task an audience-participant may choose to perform is rather different: I have significant agency when choosing to play – or not to play – this particular game. And for myself, I took satisfaction in being able to navigate the physical space and negotiate the tangle of character relationships in order to complete this task. I interacted with characters as other audience members looked on; in these moments, I felt more *participant* than *audience*. I was co-performing, however tentatively, with the actual performers. For a time, *Sleep No More* was explicitly a game, and I was playing it.

Does Bloom's idea of playable Shakespeare intercept the critiques of agency in *Sleep No More* by Hunter, Worthen, Zaiontz, and others? Not entirely. Most *Sleep No More* audience-participants do not arrive with the "information" that enables a gamified experience, whether that is knowledge of Shakespeare's text or knowledge of the "games" that it is possible to play in this performance space. For those that do, however, the impact of gamification of audience experience must be taken into consideration: gamified experiences augment audience agency and participation in ways that intercept the ambivalent evaluations of *Sleep No More* by its most critical scholars. Bloom documents a long history of thinking of theatre as game space, and in so doing her work expands the genealogy of "the immersive aesthetic" in live performance.[153] Thinking about *Sleep No More* as part of the history of playable Shakespeare makes space for an active, participatory audience role in a Shakespearean text. Gamification is part of what makes *Sleep No More* Shakespearean.

The Cinematic Imaginary and the Secret Sixth Floor

The Second Mrs. de Winter leads me through a door and into a deserted hallway. The hallway is institutional, painted gray and black. There is one overhead light; the rest of the space is in deep darkness. She sets down her suitcase a few steps away, then comes back to me. She pulls me under the light and takes both my hands. "I'm so glad you're here," she says. "You look just the same." The character welcomes me to the space by telling me, "Last night I dreamt I went to Manderley again." In her dream she could see through things. And I was there. We were together, she tells me – back at Manderley.

Mrs. de Winter leads me down the hall a few more steps and then roughly pushes me against the wall. She recounts her dream all the while, until the lights go out. In the blackout, I'm mentally out of the narrative, wondering: Am I still alone with this actor? Is someone else (a stagehand, maybe) with me now in the darkness? Another overhead light comes up abruptly: Mrs. de Winter is standing in front of me wearing a black overcoat and an early twentieth-century traveling hat. Another blackout. A brief pause in total darkness. Music and sound effects in the dark. (You'd think with nothing to look at, I'd remember what music was playing, but I can't.) Then the light comes up again, and the same actor is in the same spot in the same pose, but now she is the Sixth Floor Nurse, wearing an early twentieth-century hospital uniform, including a little white cap. It's a pretty thrilling transformation.

---

[153] Westling, *Immersion and Participation*, p. 43.

(I'm a sucker for self-consciously theatrical trickery.) This new character (though the same actor) leads me to my right, where an old-fashioned wicker and metal wheelchair awaits. Now I feel less like a long-lost lover than a patient in a haunted hospital ward. Lights must have come up gradually, revealing more of the space, because I don't recall seeing the chair when I arrived.

The Sixth Floor Nurse gestures for me to sit. I hesitate. Why? I'm an experienced theatregoer and a veteran of *Sleep No More*; I'm thrilled to be participating (at last!) in this "secret" performance, but I pause all the same. Am I *performing* hesitation? Does it seem more "in character" for me to show trepidation rather than jump in the chair with an air of "Sure! What's next?" Seeing my hesitation, the Nurse gently guides me into the chair, turns the chair around a few times (to disorient me? as a kind of ritual?), then wheels me down the hallway a short distance. Sound and music continue, and then a recorded voice begins: "Last night, I dreamt I went to Manderley again . . ." The voice-over re-performs the Second Mrs. de Winter's opening mono-logue about her dream. The Nurse turns me around in the wheelchair one last time to face the direction from which we've come; meanwhile, I'm listening to this same actor in voice-over, but in a different role. It's a compelling theatre moment. Then, releasing a mechanical lock with a loud clack, the Nurse reclines the back of the chair until I'm lying flat. Faint light begins to glow overhead, and I realize that the action of the next sequence is unfolding on the ceiling.

The voice-over continues. The actor tells a long-form version of the dream that she's back at Manderley. To my surprise, lights gradually reveal a diorama mounted *upside down* on the ceiling: I see a rural, wooded property with a winding road, as if I were floating above this landscape. Slowly a grand house can be made out. The lights come up gradually, beginning in front of me and then proceeding above me until the ceiling directly above and behind me is illuminated (if dimly). When I crane my head back, I can see the mansion and its grounds, all part of the landscape diorama on the ceiling.[154] In the moment, I think, "Oh, this must be

[154] A word on spoilers: Punchdrunk was initially reluctant to share images from *Sleep No More*. Photos of the Macbeths in their bedroom and of the banquet

Manderley!" (I admit, I had not yet seen Alfred Hitchcock's film *Rebecca* when I had my first experience of the Secret Sixth Floor. Now, in hindsight, I realize that the installation on the ceiling and the performance, both live and in voice-over, in that location offer a theatrical version of the dreamlike sequence that opens Hitchcock's 1940 film adaptation of Daphne du Maurier's 1938 novel of the same name.)

The voice-over continues as I watch the lights slowly come up: this is the dream of Manderley. After the full extent of the diorama is revealed (if dimly), the scene transitions. The recorded narration ends, darkness falls on the ceiling, and a lighting transition gradually restores my attention to the "reality" of my "right side up" space below. The back of the chair is lifted, and I'm returned to a sitting position. The Nurse wheels me back across the long, narrow room and into brighter light. She takes me by the hand and pulls me gently out of the chair. With a tug on my hand and a gesture, she directs me to the door through which we entered. She opens the door for me: I walk out alone, and she swiftly closes the door behind me. In the stairwell, I walk past the usher, who makes no sign of noticing me. I go back downstairs to the fifth floor, returning to the "normal" shared audience space of *Sleep No More*. I'm a bit dazed – pleasantly overwhelmed by the experience of this performance-within-the-performance – but I never stop walking. I know where I'm going, and I gradually pick up the pace: down another flight and straight to the Scottish village of Gallow Green; briskly down the high street, past the giant (fake) vintage poster for Scottish tourism; a left turn and along the dark, narrow corridor (the one with the

scene have been frequently reproduced in print and online since the premiere of *Sleep No More* in New York City, but for a long time few other photos were available. During and since the COVID pandemic, numerous images were posted to the *Sleep No More* Instagram feed from many locations in the performance space, including a video in which one can briefly glimpse the diorama from The Secret Sixth Floor. Additionally, The McKittrick is thoroughly described in a number of online sources (some more reliable than others). So, in describing my scholarly fieldwork on The Secret Sixth Floor in order to discuss its significance to a full appreciation of *Sleep No More*, I'm not really "spoiling" anything that hasn't already been shared by others, including Punchdrunk.

uneven brick floor and corrugated metal walls); and finally into the "Dead Bar," where Hecate is waiting for Macbeth and the witches. As audience members gather around, Hecate sits there staring at the doorway, concentrating, seemingly willing them to appear – which, in the context of *Sleep No More*'s expanded world of *Macbeth*, I presume she is. Dance music is now blasting, and The Witches' Rave is about to begin. . .

The Secret Sixth Floor of *Sleep No More* is "secret" because most who attend *Sleep No More* do not ever realize that there is a sixth floor, and among those who do, few get to see it. Access to the elusive space is granted to only a handful of audience members: periodically during each performance, a single audience member is chosen by a performer and taken alone up a flight of stairs to a separate performance space. The selection process can appear arbitrary. According to one source, *Sleep No More* performers tend not to pick audience members who seem to "want it" too much: "I rarely pick the pushy people" recounts one Punchdrunk performer, who chooses instead "the unsuspecting person, or the one who's quietly, patiently been observing you for a long while."[155] On one occasion, I witnessed an audience member walk out of the fifth-floor bathroom and blithely wander into an improvisational standoff featuring a performer and two audience members. The performer had already spent a tense minute interacting with these first audience members when she abruptly turned, grabbed Bathroom Guy, and ran up the stairs to the Sixth Floor with him while the other two (yes, I was one of them) could only watch them go. At the top of the stairs, one of the black-masked ushers who police the boundaries of *Sleep No More* silently made it clear that we could not follow. I was disappointed by the missed opportunity, but this kind of experience is a common feature of *Sleep No More*.

While Punchdrunk productions tend to be large-scale events that accommodate hundreds of audience-participants, within these large-scale productions "it is also possible to encounter clandestine one-on-ones" in which an audience member is "unmasked for a brief moment."[156] One-on-ones are distributed among the spaces and performers of *Sleep No More*. From the

---

[155] Katy Balfour, quoted in Mâchon, *The Punchdrunk Encyclopaedia*, p. 205.

[156] Mâchon, *Immersive Theatres*, p. 3.

perspective of the audience member, one-on-ones are intense experiences that seem to interrupt the narrative, literally removing the audience member from the public areas of the performance space. They "occur when coincidence of position and timing result in an audience member being taken into a smaller space with a performer to experience a short scene alone."[157] Many audience members find one-on-ones to be particularly exciting because they feel as if they've been "singled out and chosen"; certainly these "clandestine" performances are "heightened encounters," even by comparison to the experiences in the more open spaces of *Sleep No More*.[158] Each one-on-one provides a live "cinematic close up" on a single character in the context of an "intimate performance."[159] The Secret Sixth Floor experience is the most heightened, cinematic, and intimate of them all. Each of *Sleep No More*'s one-on-ones reveals something about a character or expands the "grand narratives" of the classic text that serves as the focal source material for the production (this pattern is common to other Punchdrunk productions).[160] The Secret Sixth Floor performance is something else entirely: it does not illuminate a particular character, and it is not drawn from the Shakespearean text that serves as source material for most of *Sleep No More*. Rather, this elusive scene is the culmination to the Hitchcock source material that elsewhere only supplements *Sleep No More* with cinematic references and perspectives, providing a visual and design context for the Shakespearean.

The Secret Sixth Floor is the most elaborate of *Sleep No More*'s famous one-on-one experiences. It is also a theatrical exploration of the cinematic imaginary: a live remediation of the opening of Hitchcock's *Rebecca* (upside down on the ceiling, in part), performed for an audience of one. There's a lot to unpack in the two preceding sentences. I've discussed *Sleep No More*'s one-on-ones, which are conceived by Punchdrunk not

---

[157] Biggin, *Immersive Theatre and Audience Experience*, p. 90.

[158] Mâchon, *Immersive Theatres*, p. 3; Mâchon, *The Punchdrunk Encyclopaedia*, pp. 243–44.

[159] Felix Barrett, quoted in Mâchon, *The Punchdrunk Encyclopaedia*, p. 242; Wilson, "New Ways of Seeing, Feeling, Being," p. 117.

[160] Mâchon, *Immersive Theatres*, p. 3; and see Mâchon, *Punchdrunk Encyclopaedia*, pp. 272–75 on the use of classic texts as a throughline for audiences.

only as engaging, intimate performances between one actor and one audience member, but as the strategic approximation of the kind of experience you might have watching a film, including lots of close-ups. This duality allows me to shift into more theoretical terrain, addressing the importance of the term *remediation* to *Sleep No More*, and its participation in what I term the *cinematic imaginary*.

Hitchcockian narratives and influence run through and among the *Macbeth*-derived work that dominates *Sleep No More*. Characters and fragments of narrative are drawn from Hitchcock's *Rebecca*, music from *Vertigo* (1958) and other Hitchcock films contributes to significant moments, and influences from *Psycho* (1960) can be found as well. However, more important than taking inventory of Hitchcock references is recognizing the ways in which cinematic perspectives and techniques – and the very idea of cinema – are repurposed to inform and organize the audience experience of *Sleep No More*. Two superfans of the production who write collaboratively under the moniker "paisleysweets" have blogged about the significance of Hitchcock's Manderley to *Sleep No More* as a whole:

> In *Rebecca*, Manderley was a physical, almost living, reminder of a dark past and some haunting memories that the characters of the novel (and film) were unable to escape – at least, not until the entire estate burned to the ground. In *Sleep No More*, the Manderley at the McKittrick occupies a similar symbolic space.[161]

In this blog post, the paisleysweets authors offer a notable counterpoint to the many Shakespeare-focused evaluations of *Sleep No More*. The ground-floor entry to the performance venue, a long roster of peripheral characters, and

---

[161] Paisleysweets, "Once Upon a Time." Felix Barrett, Punchdrunk artistic director and the director of *Sleep No More*, uses the term *lens* to refer to "the interpretation of a textual source through . . . other works and contexts," just one of many cinematic conceits that animate and organize Punchdrunk projects. Quoted in Mâchon, *The Punchdrunk Encyclopaedia*, p. 163. See pp. 58–61 for film terms as part of Punchdrunk's creative practice.

numerous audience experiences (including the elaborate performance on the Sixth Floor) all establish the influence Hitchcock's films as source material for *Sleep No More*. In fact, the paisleysweets authors argue that *Sleep No More* is a Hitchcock adaptation informed by Shakespeare, not the other way around. This argument threatens to upend the conventional perceptions of *Sleep No More* as an adaptation of *Macbeth* with a decorative dose of Hitchcock. The narratives, characters, and locations that dominate the "citational environment" of *Sleep No More* are drawn from Shakespearean source material, if seen through the "lens" of *Rebecca* and other Hitchcock films.[162] While the paisleysweets authors' conclusion may be too broad, their claim exposes something that should be taken seriously. It is not enough to say that *Sleep No More* is a Shakespeare adaptation, period, because it is also and at the same time littered with adaptations and remediations of Hitchcockian source material. As the paisleysweets authors put it, "it is by no coincidence that each guest must pass through Manderley to get to the McKittrick."[163] Indeed, the Hitchcockian and Shakespearean source materials of *Sleep No More* are intertwined, and the full meaning of this immersive theatre performance is dependent in no small part on the interactions between them.

Thus, it becomes clear that the Manderley Bar on the ground floor of the McKittrick and the remediation of the dream that opens *Rebecca* on the Secret Sixth Floor are connected by more than just a place-name from a movie. Characters, devised narratives, performances, and, most importantly, the movements of the audience link these locations. Carina E. I. Westling's precis of *Sleep No More* includes an interpretation of the whole event based on what she identifies as its key spaces: "*Sleep No More* is based on Shakespeare's *Macbeth* woven through with elements from Hitchcock's *Vertigo* and *Rebecca* and pivots around two key areas: the ballroom, where the slow-motion banquet scene with the entire cast takes place, and Lady Macbeth's bedroom."[164] These are indeed significant locations, and they deservedly attract audience and research attention. However, I identify a different axis, one that provides an alternative structure to the spaces and narratives of *Sleep No More*. Everyone who

---

[162] Calbi, *Spectral Shakespeares*, p. 15. [163] Paisleysweets, "Once upon a Time."
[164] Westling, *Immersion and Participation*, p. 17.

attends *Sleep No More* enters through the Manderley Bar; almost no one who attends *Sleep No More* gets to the Secret Sixth Floor and its remediation of the Manderley dream sequence. The familiar, convivial entry and the elusive grand climax are directly linked by both content and concept. Together these two sites – welcoming barroom and inaccessible attic – establish the cinematic axis around which rotates a topography of movie references, music cues, film themes, and cinematic devices used in structuring audience experience throughout *Sleep No More*. Thus, in one of the most significant theatrical adaptations of Shakespeare in the twenty-first century, these cinematic sites provide the opposing poles that organize the many spaces of *Sleep No More*, despite their non-Shakespearean source.

Because of this topography of adaptation and remediation – two terms that are considered in the following pages – *Sleep No More* sits at the intersection of embodiment, theatricality, and media.[165] I am interested in thinking these terms together rather than holding them distinct. Ben Spatz uses the term *embodiment* in the widest possible sense to describe "everything that bodies can do." In a theatre context, Spatz finds that use of this term focusses attention on "the capacities of bodies" in performance.[166] Given the breadth of some conceptions of the term, it becomes all too easy to say that everything is embodied. When I use the term "embodiment" in my discussion of *Sleep No More* and other examples of immersive Shakespeare Performance, I'm talking about performance that reminds you that you have a body – particularly the you who *right there* in the audience. Of embodiment in theatrical performance, Spatz writes: "In the core examples of performance, such as theatre and theatrical dance, representation and embodiment are tightly bound together in the singularity of an event," an event that includes spectators along with performers as part of the embodied experience.[167] While every audience member has a body, not every performance invokes that body. Josephine Mâchon refers to immersive performances that bring "meaningful" attention to the bodies of

[165] A substantial body of research considers the meanings of theatricality, often contrasting it to linear narrative and media technologies. See Davis and Postlewait, *Theatricality*; and Weber, *Theatricality as Medium*.
[166] Spatz, *What a Body Can Do*, pp. 11, 14.   [167] Spatz, "Mad Lab," p. 211.

audience members and engage audience members' embodied participation in ways that make "a significant shift from the usual spectatorial role."[168] An understanding of spectatorship as an embodied practice is crucial to understanding *Sleep No More* in relationship to the discourses of Shakespeare Performance, whether we're talking about live theatre or cinematic Shakespeare.

Embodiment and *media* – like *live* and *virtual* – might seem to be incompatible terms. Diana Henderson attempts to diagnose the anxieties that seem to arise when theatre, media, and Shakespeare intersect: "the focus on *theatrical intensity as bodily presence* may be in great part a reaction ... to the larger cultural shift of attention toward more overtly mediated – especially screen – modes of performance and communication."[169] *Sleep No More* is part of this performance-and-media discourse: it engages a stage-and-screen dialectic, even though this Shakespeare Performance is without either a stage per se or anything like a screen. Synthesizing competing strands of representation, *Sleep No More* invites audience members into a theatrical space in which preconceptions about Shakespearean (linear) narrative are disrupted and latent ideas about media come to the surface. In other words, although *Sleep No More* is a performance experience that appears to be exclusively analog, physical, IRL, it is in fact also in dialogue with (and in part organized by) media structures and technologies. What I am calling *the cinematic imaginary* is the discursive space within which audience members perceive the production. It is a product both of what Punchdrunk introduces into each show and of the frames of reference that audience members bring with them to the performance. An imaginary is a shared perspective that depends on intersubjective consensus rather than on explicit discourse. Visual discourses in our culture are so overwhelmingly determined by practices of cinematic storytelling – and cinematic spectating – that these practices constitute their own imaginary in this sense. Imar de Vries describes this kind of imaginary as a technological "condition" of "our media landscape."[170] Any imaginary – be it social, scientific, or other – is a kind of secular

[168] Mâchon, "Watching," p. 40.

[169] Henderson, *Collaborations with the Past*, p. 35n42 (added emphasis).

[170] Vries, *Tantalisingly Close*, p. 21.

mythmaking, and the cinematic imaginary offers an intuitively understood grammar of narrative form.[171]

Some critics and scholars have argued that *Sleep No More* is strongly determined by the influence of video game design, but this argument can be countered with reference to a genealogy of the live performance forms that prefigure immersive theatre. Instead, I find that it is the cinematic that pervades the spaces of *Sleep No More* and strongly informs its performance practices. While Gina Bloom's research into "playable Shakespeare" shows the value of considering the "gamification" of Shakespeare Performance, game design should not be seen as a primary influence on the conception and design of *Sleep No More* – not compared to the long histories of theatre innovation and the cinematic imaginary on this performance. This historical perspective counters claims that frame immersive productions like *Sleep No More* as merely importing digital media. There are those who argue that *Sleep No More* is simply the product of video game culture. Bloom herself responds to such claims, arguing that "their emphasis on interactivity as a digital phenomenon is at best limiting and, at worst, misleading."[172] There are competing opinions in this discourse, but the immersive aesthetic has a long genealogy – whether one is talking about *Sleep No More* or a Jacobean court masque – that cannot be reduced to video games. From a historical perspective, it is clear that VR did not invent immersion and participatory experiences did not begin with video games.

The cinematic imaginary informs much of *Sleep No More*, especially the relationships its audience constructs: with the performers, with locations, and even with movement within the immersive environment

---

[171] The term *imaginary* emerged in philosophy and sociology. For a summary of "the intellectual history and contemporary uses of *the imaginary*," see Strauss, "The Imaginary," p. 322 (original emphasis).

[172] Bloom, *Gaming the Stage*, p. 4. For selected voices in this debate, see Hopkins, "A Concise Introduction to Immersive Theatre"; Westling, *Immersion and Participation*; Worthen, "Interactive, Immersive, Original Shakespeare."; Masters, "Site and Seduction"; and Biggin, *Immersive Theatre and Audience Experience*, pp. 43–50.

of its distributed narrative. *Sleep No More*'s employment of the cinematic occasionally manifests in acts of remediation (theatrical re-performances of cinematic source material) and in cinematic signifying practices (performance experiences that approximate the moviegoing experience, like close-ups, zooms, and other cinematographic techniques). Punchdrunk draws on the cinematic imaginary in many of its productions, even while those productions reinforce that very cinematic imaginary in a representational feedback loop. References to framing and camerawork don't really describe what a theatre spectator does, even in immersive theatre, yet "citations" from classic cinema are useful points of reference for an audience that is likely to have more familiarity with the screen arts than the theatre. Of Punchdrunk's 2013 immersive production *The Drowned Man*, director Barrett says, "The audience is the camera floating around this dream." He adds, "The mask enables them to become the camera."[173] Rose Biggin cites Barrett when describing the role of cinema in Punchdrunk productions: she observes that "film is invoked regarding the show's environment and the means to engage with that environment: the creation of a fictional space with a 'cinematic' level of detail and the invitation to navigate it with 'director's cut' approach," retaining a degree of autonomy in what one chooses to frame and linger over.[174] Barrett frequently refers to cinema for comparisons to live theatre spectatorship. Of course, Hollywood and the film industry are partly the subject of *The Drowned Man*, so the analogy seems particularly apt in this case. But this cinematic analogy is not merely a vocabulary that Punchdrunk creatives use when developing scenes and shaping productions, and it does more than merely provide a frame for thinking about specific Punchdrunk performances: it introduces a technique, if not technology, into the performance. An audience member immersed in the Secret Sixth Floor is not just looking at a scene from a movie, they are on the inside of the cinematic.

The Secret Sixth Floor provides a powerful demonstration of the way the cinematic works as both subject and shaping force in *Sleep No More*.

---

[173] Quoted in Biggin, *Immersive Theatre*, p. 199.

[174] Biggin, *Immersive Theatre and Audience Experience*, p. 199.

The Secret Sixth Floor performance is a live, embodied theatrical dialogue with the flickering, prerecorded images of film. But what is explicit in the Secret Sixth Floor is implicit throughout the whole of *Sleep No More*. Characters from *Rebecca* leak downstairs; Hitchcockian figures follow paths that intersect narratively and performatively with characters and storylines from *Macbeth*. The important takeaway from this description and analysis of my Secret Sixth Floor experience is that this location reveals representational and performance strategies that are latent throughout the entire production. The "secret" that the Secret Sixth Floor keeps hidden, literally and figuratively, is *remediation*.

Performance and / as Remediation

Even though no media technology is visible in this production, I find that *Sleep No More* is subtly but pervasively engaged with media forms. This counter-intuitive perspective is shared by Paul Masters who sees in *Sleep No More* a performance that "has the potential to explore the anxious interplay of technology and site, time and space, real and virtual."[175] His conclusion reinforces my own view of *Sleep No More* as a laboratory for inquiry into the intersection of performance and media, with Shakespeare as the medium and the audience as researchers into its "potential" significance. Punchdrunk and the Wooster Group both stage performances that feature a network of references across media, though this transmedia engagement is explicit in the Wooster Group's *Hamlet* (mentioned earlier), while it is rendered largely invisible in *Sleep No More*. Nevertheless, both adaptations "seek to represent subject matter represented by other media."[176] Indeed, both adaptations are engaged in what Jay David Bolter and Richard Grusin call "remediation."

Bolter and Grusin's *Remediation: Understanding New Media* (1999) has become a foundational text in media studies and the digital humanities. The authors define remediation simply as "the representation of one medium in another" and assert that "remediation is a defining characteristic of the new

[175] Masters, "Site and Seduction," p. 44.
[176] Elliott, "The Theory of BADaptation," p. 20.

digital media."[177] The focus of *Remediation* is television, but Bolter and Grusin are at pains to link their subject to a history of media and media innovation, citing examples from art history and cinema, along with peripheral engagements with video games and the VR experiences emerging in the late twentieth century. Although most of their examples are drawn from traditional media, new media is their focus; and Bolter and Grusin insist that understanding new media is essential to understanding the future of "old" media: "What is new about new media comes from the particular ways in which they refashion older media and the ways in which older media refashion themselves to answer the challenges of new media." The examples of "older media" that are cited by Bolter and Grusin focus on visual art or film and do not include theatre, but the occasional reference to live "rock productions" provides a glimpse of how the authors imagine remediation at work in the embodied spaces of live performance: "by entering into an immediate relationship with the media themselves—the sound, the lights, the televised images—rock fans achieve an experience they regard as authentic." The perceived authenticity of such a mediatized performance redefines the real "in terms of the viewer's experience."[178] Similarly Barrett, Doyle, and the Punchdrunk creative team can be seen to refashion theatre in response to new media, including drawing heavily on the "old" new medium of cinema for both its references and signifying practices.

Sleep No More is "old media" refashioned in response to new media, in part by drawing on theatre's long history and signifying practices. Thus, it sits at the intersection of the media practices described two decades ago by Bolter and Grusin: an analog experience that is, paradoxically, deeply engaged with media culture. Shakespeare studies, surprisingly, is a field in which many scholars seem eager to set aside the "problem" of live theatre in order to focus on more stable media like literature and film, even when theatre remains a point of historical reference, given Shakespeare's association with it. The cinematic lurks beneath the surface of Punchdrunk's immersive theatre so persistently that I can well believe Barrett's claim:

---

[177] Bolter and Grusin, *Remediation*, p. 45. Numerous studies have supplemented and critiqued Bolter and Grusin. See Stiegler, *The 360° Gaze*.

[178] Bolter and Grusin, *Remediation*, pp. 15, 71, 53.

there is ample evidence that Barrett often imagines Punchdrunk's worlds as cinematic experiences.[179] It's crucial to me, though, that immersive theatre in general and Punchdrunk's performances in particular not be reduced to the poor cousin of any one media – they are dynamic performances that thrive on liveness.

While the subtle relationship between media and performance may go unnoticed by many audience-participants, it is a continual, latent presence in *Sleep No More*. Jennifer Parker-Starbuck uses the phrase "abject technology" to describe "the absence of visible or prominent technology" in a performance that is nevertheless strongly informed by technology. The same phrase can also refer to "the decision to conceptually point to this absence" of "mechanical, digital, computerized objects" in performance. For Parker-Starbuck, "to include the abject then, is to unsettle an established notion of . . . order" and to make space for technology "to remember the bodies."[180] Although there are no obvious media (like projections) in *Sleep No More*, nor visible presence of media technology, both the aesthetic construction of the performance and the audience-participant's experience as spectator of that performance, are influenced by film history, the narrative practices of cinema, and remediation. Thus, the cinematic is "abject" in *Sleep No More*: media (both "old" and new) subtend significant portions of *Sleep No More*, operating on a conceptual level rather than a visible, material one. The cinematic imaginary influences the experience while rarely overtly signaling its presence. All the references to a select set of films – Hitchcock mostly, and a Lynch or two – are traces of the subtle influence of the abject presence of the cinematic at work in the narratives, the space, and the spectators' experience of *Sleep No More*.

This structuring of experience by the subtle influence of abject media is remediation at work. As Bolter and Grusin remind their readers, "repurposing" a story is common in adaptation (even without "conscious interplay between media"), but that does not constitute remediation: "The content has been borrowed, but the medium has not been appropriated."[181]

---

[179] See Dowling, "On Cinematic Characters," *Encyclopaedia*, pp. 59 – 61. See also the citation for "cinematic" in the *Encyclopaedia*.

[180] Parker-Starbuck, "Cyborg Returns," p. 70.

[181] Bolter and Grusin, *Remediation*, pp. 45, 44.

In contrast, in *Sleep No More*, the many citations from the films of Hitchcock serve as signposts to the presence of the cinematic imaginary and underscore the value of abject technology to its spaces of performance. The surreptitious influence of abject media is a constant: from the familiar structures of traditional Hollywood melodrama to the spectator's experience of cinematic techniques (close-up, blackout, jump cut). Most of the time, I am an audience-participant with agency in my performance experience, but at other times, my perspective is the strategic approximation of what Bolter and Grusin call "the subjective camera" (this is another affordance that the masks can provide): I see exactly the scene that the director wants to show, an act of remediation that makes me "aware of the film as medium," even in the absence of that medium.[182] The strictly regulated gaze of the Secret Sixth Floor experience is the clearest example of remediation in *Sleep No More*: the site at which the force of the cinematic becomes something more than abject, more than "imaginary": the Sixth Floor one-on-one not only reenacts part of a non-Shakespearean film, it is the longest sustained example of remediation in an immersive theatre experience dependent on it.

The persistent influence of abject media is essential to an understanding of *Sleep No More*, because it helps explain the role of the cinematic in structuring audience experience. In a particularly compelling passage in *Remediation*, Bolter and Grusin write: "the experience of media is the subject of remediation."[183] Accordingly, *Sleep No More* – this seemingly analog, IRL performance – engages audiences in dynamic, nonlinear, participatory experience, an experience that is characteristic of new media. The cinematic imaginary that informs much of *Sleep No More*, especially relations between audience-participants and the performers themselves, occasionally manifests in acts of remediation: live theatrical performances of cinematic source material and the signifying practices of (new) media. Participation in *Sleep No More* includes the epistemological labor induced by an admixture of old and new theatrical forms as well as engagements with new media technologies. To put it another way, *doing things with media*

---

[182] Bolter and Grusin, *Remediation*, p. 152.
[183] Bolter and Grusin, *Remediation*, p. 59.

is remediation, and the *Sleep No More* audience is doing things with media – even if those media aren't always visible.

Criticisms and Counternarratives

The preceding has focused on *Sleep No More* as Shakespeare, as performance, as adaptation, as remediation. But *Sleep No More* is also a business, and there are pragmatic issues to consider, too. The production has drawn criticism for its commercial marketing; and *Sleep No More* New York has been criticized for its workplace practices.

In a 2015 article that provides an early history of *Sleep No More*, Alexis Soloski cites key complaints about the production, including a contention that "the fragmented nature of the storytelling" is merely a marketing device calculated to encourage repeat attendance. To her credit, Soloski concludes that this fragmentary narrative is an aesthetic device, not an entrepreneurial gimmick.[184] Indeed, most theatre specialists would roll their eyes at this criticism: nonlinear narratives have been a commonplace of postdramatic theatre for decades. Indeed, an innovation of *Sleep No More* as an immersive adaptation is to distribute Shakespeare's tragedy across a large, multistory performance space. More to the point of this criticism, though, Punchdrunk began to update the space regularly following the initial enthusiastic audience response to the New York production, "to seed the rooms with surprises for dedicated audience members," which the company saw as "a way to reward repeat visits."[185] The choice to regularly revise design in small ways gave rise to claims that Punchdrunk's "money-grabbing touches" begin with the ticket pricing and "extend all the way into the show."[186] There are those critics (like Prince and Zaiontz, noted previously) who argue that in both design and practice, Punchdrunk is encouraging a competitive (even aggressive) gamification of the *Sleep No More* experience. Megan Reilly found, on a return visit to *Sleep No More*, that "gameplay mechanics had essentially overtaken the art." However,

---

[184] Soloski, "*Sleep No More*: From Avant Garde Theatre."

[185] Soloski, "*Sleep No More* Awakens."

[186] Miriam Gillinson, quoted in "*Sleep No More*: From Avant Garde Theatre."

despite ambivalences about *Sleep No More*, Reilly remains engaged with the idea of live, gamified immersive experiences in the belief that "understanding what draws people to games can be used to draw in audiences that might not attend traditional theatre."[187]

The most common subject for criticism of *Sleep No More* is to be found not in the performance itself but in its marketing and in the commercial capitalization of the long-running New York venue. Increasingly, audiences are being drawn to immersive events that have been produced specifically to support corporate marketing campaigns and product launches – from Secret Cinema events based on forthcoming films to cruise ship entertainment. The degree to which an immersive event is perceived to pursue an explicitly mercenary goal as part of the experience economy is often the degree to which it is perceived to eschew an artistic mission. Accordingly, *Sleep No More*'s long commercial run in New York and the launch of its satellite production in Shanghai are perceived by some as purely revenue-driven. The company's addition of a *Sleep No More*-themed restaurant at the New York location is one example of Punchdrunk's theme park-ification of the site; and the company's profitable collaborations with corporate sponsors have done nothing to discourage criticism.[188] Kathryn Prince articulates the origin of the critical discontent, in an otherwise polemical discussion: "There was an experimental, edgy, risky aura to *Sleep No More* when I saw it early in its run. The goods on display were exclusively in service of the production ... A year later, Punchdrunk had capitalized on the marketing niches its successful production had uncovered."[189] In other words, *Sleep No More* began as the kind of experimental Shakespeare adaptation that would engage and excite many theatre researchers. Thus, the ire directed by many scholars and passionate theatregoers toward an experimental production that is also a commercial success seems to emerge in part from audience expectations, including the expectation that participatory

---

[187] Reilly, "Learning from the Gamification of Theater."

[188] More altruistically, Punchdrunk Enrichment provides educational programming for UK schools and training for UK-based instructors.

[189] Prince, "Intimate and Epic," p. 255.

performance will model "the co-creation of meaningful 'IRL' moments" while remaining "a refuge from commodification."[190] While the performance itself is still much the same as the one that attracted the attention of Prince and other scholars, the production company's adoption of an aggressive approach to marketing and has repelled many specialists who were initially champions of Punchdrunk.

Recent journalistic reporting offers a particularly sharp critique of *Sleep No More*, one that should impact all immersive theatre and participatory performance. Soloski sums up this critique in a piercing quip: "it's the unusual avant-garde show that could double as a bachelor party destination."[191] While one may cheer when a company making work outside the mainstream finds success, the intimate performances and erotic content of *Sleep No More* are part of the appeal to audience members, some of whom have been abusive toward performers. Similar behavior was reported during the Museum of Modern Art retrospective of performance artist Marina Abramović, *The Artist Is Present* (2010). Some of Abramović's works were reperformed as part of the retrospective, and nude performance artists reported harassment, including physical assaults. If such criminal misconduct can happen in the wide-open, well-lit galleries of a white-walled museum, it should be no surprise that it could occur in the dark passages of *Sleep No More* as well. However, Emursive, the production company behind *Sleep No More*'s commercial incarnation in New York, seems initially to have been unprepared to provide for the safety of its performers.

When *Sleep No More* premiered in New York, in an effort to encourage participation in and exploration of the "dreamlike world" of the McKittrick, Punchdrunk's focus was on encouraging audiences to drop their inhibitions. The language around mask-wearing is a case in point. As Barrett explains, the masks "allow people to be more selfish and more voyeuristic then they might normally be. Hidden behind a fictional layer, they lose some of their inhibitions."[192] Punchdrunk has been criticized for not doing enough to

---

[190] Paryzer, "Playable Plays."

[191] Soloski, "The Problem with Immersive Theatre."

[192] Barrett, quoted in *Sleep No More* program, p. 24.

discourage behavior by those selfish and voyeuristic audience members some of whom have disrupted performances and abused performers. In response, language was added to *Sleep No More*'s pre-show "elevator speech." These instructions have always included the requirement that audience members keep their masks on and remain silent at all times; now they include an in-character exhortation from a costumed host to respect the personal space of performers. Additional black-masked ushers were added to the performance space; protocols were introduced to support actors during the performance and to identify audience members who need to be removed; and a system was established for reporting incidents after the fact. Still, as recently as 2018, Emursive and Punchdrunk representatives seemed to resist taking full responsibility for performer safety.[193] These management failures left a negative impression of *Sleep No More* as a workplace, an impression that reflected on the production itself.

However, in the wake of the pandemic, attention to performer well-being has led to changes, including redesigned masks that incorporated N95 face coverings and a temporary pause on one-on-ones. Casting for *Sleep No More* New York is clearly more inclusive; and for the latest Punchdrunk production, *The Burnt City*, the company enlisted an intimacy coordinator during the production process, and subsequently instituted behavior and safety protocols for performance. These management responses suggest a company-wide adoption of more respectful production practices.[194]

Conclusion

At one point in her loop, Lady Macbeth walks along the steamer trunks that line the perimeter of the Macbeths' suite. She ignores the audience – we're just ghosts in her bedroom, witnessing her experiences unseen (usually). She climbs across the steamer trunks stacked in the corner, then exits

---

[193] See Amber Jamieson, "Performers and Staffers."

[194] Doyle states that current Punchdrunk "performers have a very strict set of actions to take should they ever feel compromised or uncomfortable." See Allfree, "Punchdrunk Interview."

Figure 9 Tori Sparks performs Lady Macbeth's "window dance." Photo: Lucas Jackson, REUTERS / Alamy Stock Photo.

through a concealed door. She reappears moments later, visible through a window about five feet off the ground. Is this meant to be a kind of walk-in closet? Or is it a performance space outside of any narrative logic? Access to this space is regulated by a black-masked usher standing in the shadows, so the audience watches from the bedroom. We can dimly view her within, performing obscure tasks. Does she change clothes? Shortly, Lady Macbeth comes forward and begins to dance on the wide ledge inside the window frame (Figure 9). This solo has a self-destructive quality, but unlike Lady Macbeth's dance on the padded bed, the window's frame is unyielding. Lady Macbeth flings herself at the window frame and then back down to the ledge of this box-like dance space. The choreography looks beautiful, visceral, and grueling – much like the work of Elizabeth Streb, from whose choreography this dance is adapted.

Versions of Streb's dance solo "Little Ease" (1985) can be seen online.[195] The similarity with Lady Macbeth's "window dance" is striking.

---

[195] See "Streb / Ringside: *Little Ease*," Jacobs Pillow Dance Festival digital archive.

We might call Lady Macbeth's performance an adaptation or perhaps a reperformance; or, this dance could be seen as citing or quoting Streb's choreography; or, it simply could be taken as an homage to "Little Ease."[196] I have seen this dance several times with different performers in the role: each actor-dancer who plays Lady Macbeth brings a slightly different approach to this demanding dance. The piece seems to be about guilt and regret, or perhaps about feeling trapped – indeed, Streb's title refers to a medieval English prison cell. The moment invites interpretation as a choreographic expression of Lady Macbeth's character. This is also one of two performances in *Sleep No More* that explicitly seek to reproduce a cinematic experience: we watch Lady Macbeth's dance through a wide, rectangular window that resembles the frame of a movie screen. *Sleep No More* choreographer Maxine Doyle says that she explicitly seeks out such moments, asking her dancers "to find frames – like doorways, windows, corners, and mirrors, and to create images in the frames." As Doyle explains, this is one of her many media-influenced techniques for making choreography: "The effect for the viewer is immediately cinematic."[197] Today, "Little Ease" can be seen on recorded video, but Lady Macbeth's window dance forcefully brings embodiment back to a classic of contemporary dance in a way that reminds us that while it endures on screens, "framed" in the digital archive, it does so as a document of a famously demanding live performance.

The relationship between a dancer and choreography only seems uncomplicated, and Lady Macbeth's window dance reveals a particularly complex relationship among choreography, embodied performance, digital media, and the cinematic imaginary. It's a dance based on another dance that is best known from video footage; and it is also a dance seen through a frame that makes this live dance look as if it were itself on a screen. What we see in this scene is, among other things, an act of remediation – the refashioning of new media in the context of "old media"

---

[196] My thanks to choreographer and dancer Jessica Humphrey for directing me to "Little Ease."

[197] Quoted in Mâchon, *The Punchdrunk Encyclopaedia*, p. 105, and see p. 51.

forms.[198] For those who can see the ghostly traces, Lady Macbeth's physically challenging window dance is framed (literally and figuratively) by media technologies. This one dance sequence is constituted by a dynamic set of mutually informing live and mediatized influences – but in the complexity of its choreography and directing it is not exceptional; rather, it is representative. The same can be said for much of *Sleep No More*: uncanny spectatorship surfaces a network of references, including media histories as well as Shakespearean textuality.

Alexis Soloski revisited *Sleep No More* on the occasion of its reopening in 2022 after closure during the pandemic; I, too, have seen it since reopening.[199] We both found that this long-running, gamified performance, despite criticism from some quarters, remains an experience that many audience-participants find intensely satisfying, intellectually stimulating, and, in a word, *fun*. Along with "immersive" and "Shakespeare," "fun" is another keyword for *Sleep No More*. Just because an immersive experience may be fun doesn't negate its critical value. Not all fun is frivolous. Sociologist Adam Grant juxtaposes "the shallow fun of frivolous activities" with "the deep fun of creating together and solving problems together."[200] In the case of *Sleep No More*, it's a species of fun produced by old theatrical forms entangled with the long genealogy of immersive performance and the emergent perspectives of new media technology. This kind of fun is essential to *Sleep No More*'s ability to function as an epistemological process, as a mode of critical inquiry, as a "strange tool" for producing new knowledges, or, in Johanna Drucker's phrase, as an example of "knowledge as performance and invention."[201] The result is a Shakespeare adaptation that addresses real-world problematics through a hauntological immersive theatre experience.

In *Sleep No More*, I find (strange) tools for critical inquiry into Shakespeare Performance, audience experience, and contemporary culture. As this Element goes to press, *Sleep No More* is (theatre) history. On the first

[198] Bolter and Grusin, *Remediation*, p. 15, and see pp. 15–19.

[199] Soloski, "*Sleep No More* Awakens."

[200] Grant, "There's a Specific Kind of Joy We've Been Missing."

[201] Drucker, *Graphesis*, p. 197.

page of the introduction, I note that *Sleep No More* is closing. I began writing this book with the intent that it would be a tool for present-day audience-participants. Instead, this mini-monograph has become the first retrospective on *Sleep No More*: what it *was* and how it *worked* (past tense). Shakespeare's body of work continues to inspire new thinking about embodied spaces, media, and textuality because no other cultural resource offers scholars, artists, and (uncanny) spectators the opportunity to engage with four hundred years of previous thinking about these subjects: adaptation, remediation, ghosts, and, of course, performance.

Bibliography

Allfree, Claire. "Punchdrunk Interview: 'Audiences Are Human – They Sometimes Misbehave." *Telegraph* (March 22, 2022).

Als, Hilton. "Shadow and Act," review of *Sleep No More*. *New Yorker* (May 2, 2011).

Aronson, Arnold. *The History and Theory of Environmental Scenography* (Michigan: University of Michigan Press, 1981).

Barrett, Brian. "*Pokemon Go* and *Sleep No More* Creators Are Teaming Up on AR." *Wired* (June 30, 2020).

Bay-Cheng, Sarah. "Theater Is Media: Some Principles for a Digital Historiography of Performance." *Theater*, 42.2 (2012), 27–41.

Bay-Cheng, Sarah, Jennifer Parker-Starbuck, and David Z. Saltz (eds.). *Performance and Media: Taxonomies for a Changing Field* (Ann Arbor: University of Michigan Press, 2015).

Bennett, Susan. *Theatre Audiences: A Theory of Production and Reception*, 2nd ed. (London: Routledge, 1997).

Biggin, Rose. *Immersive Theatre and Audience Experience: Space, Game, and Story in the Work of Punchdrunk* (New York: Palgrave Macmillan, 2017).

Bishop, Claire. *Artificial Hells: Participatory Art and the Politics of Spectatorship* (New York: Verso, 2012).

Blau, Herbert. *Take Up the Bodies: Theater at the Vanishing Point* (Urbana: University of Illinois Press, 1982).

Bleeker, Maaike. "What If This Were an Archive? Abstraction, Enactment and Human Implicatedness." In Maaike Bleeker (ed.), *Transmission in Motion: The Technologizing of Dance* (London: Routledge, 2016), pp. 199–214.

Bloom, Gina. *Gaming the Stage: Playable Media and the Rise of English Commercial Theatre* (Ann Arbor: University of Michigan Press, 2018).

Bloom, Gina, Anston Bosman, and William N. West. "Ophelia's Intertheatricality, or How Performance Is History." *Theatre Journal*, 65.2 (2013), pp. 165–82.

Bolter, Jay David, and Richard Grusin. *Remediation: Understanding New Media* (Cambridge, MA: MIT Press, 1999).

Brantley, Ben. "Shakespeare Slept Here, Albeit Fitfully," review of *Sleep No More. New York Times* (April 13, 2011).

"Why I'll Never Stop Being a Theater Critic." *New York Times* (October 13, 2020).

Bulman, James C. "Introduction: Cross-Currents in Performance Criticism." *The Oxford Handbook of Shakespeare and Performance.* (2017), pp. 1–9.

Burt, Richard (ed.). *Shakespeare After Mass Media* (New York: Palgrave Macmillan, 2000).

Calbi, Maurizio. *Spectral Shakespeares: Media Adaptations in the Twenty-First Century* (New York: Palgrave Macmillan, 2013).

Carlson, Marvin. *The Haunted Stage: The Theatre as Memory Machine* (Ann Arbor: University of Michigan Press, 2001).

Cartmell, Deborah. "Film as the New Shakespeare and Film on Shakespeare: Reversing the Shakespeare/Film Trajectory." *Literature Compass* 3.5 (August 25, 2006): pp. 1150–59.

Chansky, Dorothy. "A Concise Introduction to Audience." *Digital Theatre+* (2021), www.digitaltheatreplus.com

Cook, Amy. *Building Character: The Art and Science of Casting* (Ann Arbor: University of Michigan Press, 2018).

Davis, Tracy C. and Thomas Postlewait. *Theatricality* (New York: Cambridge University Press, 2003).

Davis, Tracy C. and Peter W. Marx. "Introduction: On Critical Media History." In Tracy C. Davis and Peter W. Marx (eds.), *The Routledge*

Companion to Theatre and Performance Historiography. (Routledge, 2021), pp. 1–39.

Derrida, Jacques. *Specters of Marx: The State of the Debt, the Work of Mourning and the New International*. Trans. Peggy Kamuf (Routledge, 1994).

DesRochers, Rick. "Immersive Performance and Sensory Stimulation: The Intimacy of Participation in Third Rail Projects' Then She Fell." *Coup de Théâtre* [journal] 35 (2021). *Special Issue: Anglophone and Francophone Approaches to Immersive Theatre* (Le théâtre immersif sur les scenes contemporaines anglophones et francophones), pp. 173–90.

Dinesh, Nandita. *Memos from a Theatre Lab: Exploring What Immersive Theatre "Does."* (New York: Routledge, 2017).

Dixon, Steve. *Digital Performance: A History of New Media in Theatre, Dance, Performance Art, and Installation* (Cambridge, MA: MIT Press, 2007).

Drucker, Johanna. *Graphesis: Visual Forms of Knowledge Production* (Cambridge, MA: Harvard University Press, 2014).

Eglinton, Andrew. "Reflections on a Decade of Punchdrunk Theatre." *TheatreForum* 37 (2010), pp. 46–55.

Elliott, Kamilla. "The Theory of BADaptation." In Dennis Cutchins, Katja Krebs, and Eckart Voigts (eds.), *The Routledge Companion to Adaptation* (London: Routledge, 2018), pp. 18–27.

Ferdman, Bertie. *Off Sites: Contemporary Performance Beyond Site-Specific* (Southern Illinois University Press, 2018).

Freshwater, Helen. *Theatre & Audience* (New York: Palgrave Macmillan, 2009).

Galey, Alan. *The Shakespearean Archive* (Cambridge: Cambridge University Press, 2014).

Gardner, Lyn. "Immersive Theatre & Performance." *Digital Theatre+* (n.d.), www.digitaltheatreplus.com

"Welcome to Fallow Cross: Inside the Secret Village Built by Punchdrunk." *Guardian* (April 25, 2017).

Giesekam, Greg. *Staging the Screen: The Use of Film and Video in Theatre* (New York: Palgrave Macmillan, 2007).

Gillinson, Miriam. "Punchdrunk's *Sleep No More*: Is This a Sell-Out Which I See before Me?" *Guardian* (February 6, 2012).

Grant, Adam. "There's a Specific Kind of Joy We've Been Missing." *New York Times* (July 10, 2021).

Guneratne, Anthony R. "'Thou Dost Usurp Authority': Beerbohm Tree, Reinhardt, Olivier, Welles, and the Politics of Adapting Shakespeare." In Diana Henderson (ed.), *A Concise Companion to Shakespeare on Screen* (Malden, MA: Blackwell, 2006), pp. 31–53.

Harvie, Jen. "Agency and Complicity in 'A Special Civic Room': London's Tate Modern Turbine Hall." In D. J. Hopkins, Shelley Orr, Kim Solga (eds.), *Performance and the City* (New York: Palgrave, 2009).

Henderson, Diana. *Collaborations with the Past: Reshaping Shakespeare across Time and Media* (Ithaca, NY: Cornell University Press, 2018).

Hodgdon, Barbara. "Re-Incarnations." In Pascale Aebischer, Edward J. Esche, and Nigel Wheale (eds.), *Remaking Shakespeare: Performance across Media, Genres and Cultures* (New York: Palgrave Macmillan, 2003), pp. 190–209.

"Scholar Spotlight: Barbara Hodgdon." (Interview) By D. J. Hopkins. *ATHENews* 22.8 (June 16, 2008).

Hodgdon, Barbara. *Shakespeare, Performance, and the Archive*. (Routledge, 2016).

Holland, Peter. "Haunting Shakespeare, or King Lear Meets Alice." In Mary Luckhurst and Emilie Morin (eds.), *Theatre and Ghosts: Materiality, Performance, and Modernity* (New York: Palgrave Macmillan, 2014), pp. 197–216.

Hopkins, D. J. "A Concise Introduction to Immersive Theatre." *Digital Theatre +* (2022), www.digitaltheatreplus.com.

"Hamlet's Mirror Image: Theatre, Film, and the Shakespearean Imaginary." *Journal of Dramatic Theory and Criticism*, 29.1 (2014), pp. 7–24.

"Reconsidering the Boredom of King James: Performance and Premodern Histories." *Journal of Medieval and Early Modern Studies*, 51.3 (September 2021), pp. 477–86.

"Research, Counter-Text, Performance: Reconsidering the (Textual) Authority of the Dramaturg." *Theatre Topics*, 13.1 (2003), pp. 1–17.

Review of *Sleep No More*. *Theatre Journal*, 64.2 (2012), pp. 269–71.

Hopkins, D. J., Shelley Orr, and Kim Solga (eds.). *Performance and the City* (New York: Palgrave Macmillan, 2009).

Hopkins, D. J., and Kim Solga (eds.). *Performance and the Global City* (New York: Palgrave Macmillan, 2013).

Hunter, E. B. "Enactive Spectatorship, Critical Making, and Dramaturgical Analysis: Building *Something Wicked*, the *Macbeth* Video Game." *International Journal of Performance Arts and Digital Media*, 16.1 (2020), pp. 1–17.

Hunter, E. B. Presentation, Digital Shakespeares lecture series, San Diego State University (virtual), October 1, 2020.

Jamieson, Amber. "Performers and Staffers at Sleep No More Say Audience Members Have Sexually Assulted Them." *Buzzfeed* (February 6, 2018).

Judge, Alysia. "'Playable Shows Are the Future': What Punchdrunk Theatre Learned from Games." *Guardian* (February 8, 2019).

Kaye, Nick. *Site-Specific Art: Performance, Place and Documentation* (London: Routledge, 2000).

Kennedy, Dennis. "The Spectator, the Text, and Ezekiel." In David Schalkwyk (ed.), *The Shakespearean International Yearbook*, vol. 10, *Special Section: The Achievement of Robert Weimann* (Farnham: Ashgate, 2010), pp. 39–46.

Kidnie, Margaret Jane. *Shakespeare and the Problem of Adaptation* (London: Routledge, 2009).

Knowles, Ric. "The Death of a Chief: Watching for Adaptation; or, How I Learned to Stop Worrying and Love the Bard." In Barbara Hodgdon (ed.), "*Watching Ourselves Watching Shakespeare I*," special issue, *Shakespeare Bulletin*, 25.3 (2007), pp. 53–65.

Lehmann, Hans-Thies. *Postdramatic Theatre* (London: Routledge, 2006).

Levin, Laura. *Performing Ground: Space, Camouflage and the Art of Blending In* (New York: Palgrave Macmillan, 2014).

Lin, T. Erika. *Shakespeare and the Materiality of Performance* (New York: Palgrave Macmillan, 2012).

Luckhurst, Mary, and Emilie Morin. "Introduction: Theatre and Spectrality." In Mary Luckhurst and Emilie Morin (eds.), *Theatre and Ghosts: Materiality, Performance, and Modernity* (New York: Palgrave Macmillan, 2014), pp. 1–23.

(eds.). *Theatre and Ghosts: Materiality, Performance, and Modernity* (New York: Palgrave Macmillan, 2014).

Lukowski, Andrzej. "Punchdrunk Comes Home with 'The Burnt City.'" *Time Out London* (March 29, 2022).

Mâchon, Josephine. *Immersive Theatres: Intimacy and Immediacy in Contemporary Performance* (New York: Palgrave Macmillan, 2013).

(ed.). *The Punchdrunk Encyclopaedia* (London: Routledge, 2019).

"Watching, Attending, Sense-Making: Spectatorship in Immersive Theatres." *Journal of Contemporary Drama in English*, 4.1 (2016), pp. 34–48.

Marvin, Carolyn. *When Old Technologies Were New: Thinking about Electric Communication in the Late Nineteenth Century* (Oxford: Oxford University Press, 1990).

Masters, Paul. "Site and Seduction: Space, Sensuality, and Use-Value in the Immersive Theater." In Josh Machamer (ed.), *Immersive Theatre: Engaging the Audience* (Champaign, IL: Common Ground Research Networks, 2017), pp. 17–44.

Nakamura, Jessica. "Against the Flows of Theory: Expanding the Ghost with Japanese Noh." *Journal of Dramatic Theory and Criticism*, 35.2 (2021), pp. 151–69.

Noë, Alva. *Strange Tools: Art and Human Nature* (New York: Hill and Wang, 2015).

Orgel, Stephen. *The Authentic Shakespeare and Other Problems of the Early Modern Stage* (London: Routledge, 2002).

paisleysweets. "All There Is: The Music of the McKittrick Hotel." *Back to Manderley*, blog (January 26, 2013), https://paisleysweets.tumblr .com/post/41572547344/.

　"Once upon a Time, There Was a Little Boy. He Was the Happiest Little Boy in the Whole World … " *Back to Manderley*, blog (June 13, 2013), https://paisleysweets.tumblr.com/post/52892400078/.

Parker-Starbuck, Jennifer. "Cyborg Returns: Always-Already Subject Technologies." In Sarah Bay-Cheng, Jennifer Parker-Starbuck, and David Z. Saltz (eds.), *Performance and Media: Taxonomies for a Changing Field* (Ann Arbor: University of Michigan Press, 2015), pp. 65–92.

　Cyborg Theatre: Corporeal/Technological Intersections in Multimedia Performance (New York: Palgrave Macmillan, 2011).

Paryzer, Drew. "Playable Plays: Toward a New Interactivity." *Howlround Theatre Commons* (July 18, 2022), https://howlround.com/playable-plays-toward-new-interactivity.

Postlewait, Thomas. "Historiography and the Theatrical Event: A Primer with Twelve Cruxes." *Theatre Journal* 43.2 (1991), pp. 157–78.

Pressman, Jessica. *Digital Modernism: Making It New in New Media* (New York: Oxford University Press, 2014).

Prince, Kathryn. "Intimate and Epic *Macbeth*s in Contemporary Performance." *The Oxford Handbook of Shakespeare and Performance*, (2017), pp. 250–63.

Rayner, Alice. *Ghosts: Death's Double and the Phenomena of Theatre* (Minneapolis: University of Minnesota Press, 2006).

Reilly, Megan. "Learning from the Gamification of Theater." *Howlround Theatre Commons* (June 18, 2014), https://howlround.com/learning-gamification-theater.

Ridout, Nicholas. *Theatre & Ethics* (New York: Palgrave Macmillan, 2009).

Riordan, Kevin. "Ghosts—in Theory—in Theater." *Intertexts*, 18.2 (2014), pp. 165–80.

Roach, Joseph. *Cities of the Dead: Circum-Atlantic Performance* (New York: Columbia University Press, 1996).

Rouse, John. "Textuality and Authority in Theater and Drama: Some Contemporary Possibilities." In Janelle G. Reinelt and Joseph R. Roach (eds.), *Critical Theory and Performance* (Ann Arbor: University of Michigan Press, 1992), pp. 146–58.

Salvato, Nick. "Uncloseting Drama: Gertrude Stein and the Wooster Group." *Modern Drama*, 50.1 (2007), pp. 36–59.

Sanders, Julie. *Adaptation and Appropriation* (London: Routledge, 2006).

Schalkwyk, David. "Text and Performance, Reiterated: A Reproof Valiant or Lie Direct?" In David Schalkwyk (ed.), *The Shakespearean International Yearbook*, vol. 10, *Special Section: The Achievement of Robert Weimann* (Farnham: Ashgate, 2010), pp. 47–75.

Schechner, Richard. "6 Axioms for Environmental Theatre." *The Drama Review* 12 (1968), pp. 41–64.

Schneider, Rebecca. *Performing Remains: Art and War in Times of Theatrical Reenactment* (London: Routledge, 2011).

Shaughnessy, Robert. "Stage, Screen, and Nation: *Hamlet* and the Space of History." In Diana Henderson (ed.), *A Concise Companion to Shakespeare on Screen* (Malden, MA: Blackwell, 2006), pp. 54–76.

Shaw, Helen. "The Wild Invention of Fefu and Her Friends." *New York Magazine* (November 25, 2019).

Shendruk, Amanda. "An Industry Built on the Suspension of Disbelief Reveals Its Secrets to World Building." *Quartz* (January 15, 2020).

Sleep No More. Directed by Felix Barrett and Maxine Doyle. Choreographed by Maxine Doyle (New York City: Punchdrunk and Emursive, 2011; Shanghai: Punchdrunk International and SMG Live, 2016). Performance and program notes (citations in the text are to the New York program notes).

Sofer, Andrew. *Dark Matter: Invisibility in Drama, Theatre, and Performance* (Ann Arbor: University of Michigan Press, 2013).

Solga, Kim. *Theory for Theatre Studies: Space* (London: Methuen Drama, 2019).

Soloski, Alexis. "The Problem with Immersive Theatre: Why Actors Need Extra Protection from Sexual Assault." *Guardian* (February 12, 2018).

"Sleep No More: From Avant Garde Theatre to Commercial Blockbuster." *Guardian* (March 31, 2015).

"Sleep No More Awakens After a Long Hibernation." *New York Times* (February 9, 2022).

Spatz, Ben. *What a Body Can Do: Technique as Knowledge, Practice as Research* (New York: Routledge, 2015).

"Mad Lab – or Why We Can't Do Practice as Research." In Annette Arlander, Bruce Barton, Melanie Dreyer-Lude, and Ben Spatz (eds.), *Performance as Research: Knowledge, Methods, Impact* (New York: Routledge, 2018), pp. 209–23.

Stiegler, Christian. *The 360° Gaze: Immersions in Media, Society, and Culture* (Cambridge, MA: MIT Press, 2021).

Strauss, Claudia. "The Imaginary." *Anthropological Theory*, 6.3 (2006), pp. 322–44.

"Streb / Ringside: Little Ease." Jacobs Pillow Dance Festival digital archive. Accessed December 15, 2022. https://danceinteractive.jacob spillow.org/streb-ringside/little-ease/.

Temperton, James. "Punchdrunk's Next Great Act." *Wired* (December 22, 2017).

Tree, Herbert Beerbohm. *King John*. Directed by William Kennedy Laurie Dickson (London: British Mutoscope and Biograph, 1899). Silent film.

Vries, Imar O. de. *Tantalisingly Close: An Archaeology of Communication Desires in Discourses of Mobile Wireless Media* (Amsterdam: Amsterdam University Press, 2012).

Weber, Samuel. *Theatricality as Medium* (New York: Fordham University Press, 2004).

Weimann, Robert. *Author's Pen and Actor's Voice: Playing and Writing in Shakespeare's Theatre* (Cambridge: Cambridge University Press, 2000).

"Performance in Shakespeare's Theatre: Ministerial and/or Magisterial?" In David Schalkwyk (ed.), *The Shakespearean International Yearbook*, vol. 10, *Special Section*: *The Achievement of Robert Weimann* (Farnham: Ashgate, 2010), pp. 3–29.

Weimann, Robert, and Douglas Bruster. *Shakespeare and the Power of Performance: Stage and Page in the Elizabethan Theatre* (Cambridge: Cambridge University Press, 2008).

Westling, Carina E. I. *Immersion and Participation in Punchdrunk's Theatrical Worlds* (London: Methuen Drama, 2020).

Wilson, Harry Robert. "New Ways of Seeing, Feeling, Being: Intimate Encounters in Virtual Reality Performance." *International Journal of Performance Arts and Digital Media*, 16.2 (2020), pp. 114–33.

Wolf, Matt. "The Carnage of War, in Punchdrunk's New London Show." *New York Times* (April 29, 2022).

Worthen, W. B. "Antigone's Bones." *TDR: The Drama Review* 52.3 (Fall 2008), pp. 10–33.

"Interactive, Immersive, Original Shakespeare." *Shakespeare Bulletin*, 35.3 (2017), pp. 407–24.

"Shakespeare Performance Studies." In David Schalkwyk (ed.), *The Shakespearean International Yearbook*, vol. 10, *Special Section: The Achievement of Robert Weimann* (Farnham: Ashgate, 2010), pp. 77–92.

Shakespeare Performance Studies (Cambridge: Cambridge University Press, 2014).

Zaiontz, Keren. "Narcissistic Spectatorship in Immersive and One-on-One Performance." *Theatre Journal*, 66.3 (October 2014), pp. 405–25.

Acknowledgements

First, I am grateful to the editor of the Cambridge Element series, W.B. Worthen. An exceptional scholar and editor, Bill has offered me encouragement and patience while I've worked on this book, a project that seemed so straightforward prior to the pandemic. Here, I lean into some of Worthen's influential scholarship. Though I've been citing him for years, it's a pleasure to be in dialogue with his work at greater length.

At my university, thanks go to my colleagues Niyi Coker and Peter Cirino for their institutional and personal support. My university grants program provided travel and research funding over the years that made it possible for me to conduct research that included repeatedly attending a performance thousands of miles from where I live. Thanks as well to Joanna Brooks and the office for Faculty Advancement for professional and research support. I'm grateful to the anonymous external reader of this book for a warm, insightful response. And thanks to Jessica Hinds-Bond, who delivered expert copy editing and editorial advice.

I owe personal thanks to friends and colleagues who have encouraged this project and me. The list includes, but is not limited to Lauren Beck, Erika Lin, Jessica Nakamura, and Robert Weimann. Eric Smigel gave me helpful input and writing accountability at a critical stage. Becky Steinberger provided the first venue in which I presented some of these ideas; Pam Lach and Jessica Pressman provided another. Special thanks to Amy Cook, who generously read a complete draft and gave me valuable input and cheerleading. And Shelley Orr always knows just the right thing to say at just the right time, for which I am forever grateful.

Cambridge Elements ≡

Shakespeare Performance

W. B. Worthen
Barnard College

W. B. Worthen is Alice Brady Pels Professor in the Arts, and
Chair of the Theatre Department at Barnard College. He is also
co-chair of the Ph.D. Program in Theatre at Columbia
University, where he is Professor of English and Comparative
Literature.

ADVISORY BOARD

Pascale Aebischer, University of
Exeter
Todd Landon Barnes, Ramapo
College of New Jersey
Susan Bennett, University of
Calgary
Rustom Bharucha, Jawaharlal
Nehru University, New Delhi
Gina Bloom, University of
California, Davis
Bridget Escolme, Queen Mary
University of London
Alan Galey, University of Toronto
Douglas Lanier, University of
New Hampshire
Julia Reinhard Lupton, University
of California, Irvine
Peter W. Marx, University of Köln
Sonia Massai, King's College
London
Alfredo Michel Modenessi,
National Autonomous
University of Mexico
Robert Shaughnessy, Guildford
School of Acting, University of
Surrey
Ayanna Thompson, George
Washington University
Yong Li-Lan, National University
of Singapore

ABOUT THE SERIES

Shakespeare Performance is a dynamic collection in a field that is both always emerging and always evanescent. Responding to the global range of Shakespeare performance today, the series launches provocative, urgent criticism for researchers, graduate students and practitioners. Publishing scholarship with a direct bearing on the contemporary contexts of Shakespeare performance, it considers specific performances, material and social practices, ideological and cultural frameworks, emerging and significant artists and performance histories.

Cambridge Elements ☰

Shakespeare Performance

Printed in the United States
by Baker & Taylor Publisher Services